The Dragons of Autism

Autism as a Source of Wisdom

Olga Holland

Jessica Kingsley Publishers
London and Philadelphia

First published in the United Kingdom in 2003
by Jessica Kingsley Publishers Ltd
116 Pentonville Road
London N1 9JB, England
and
325 Chestnut Street
Philadelphia, PA 19106, USA
www.jkp.com

Copyright © Olga Holland 2003

Library of Congress Cataloging in Publication Data
A CIP catalog record for this book is available from the Library of Congress

British Library Cataloguing in Publication Data

Holland, Olga, 1957-
 The dragons of autism : autism as a source of wisdom / Olga Holland.
  p. cm.
 Includes bibliographical references and index.
 ISBN 1-84310-741-4 (alk paper)
  1. Autistic children--Family relationships. 2. Parents of autistic children. 3. Autism in children. I. Title.

 RJ506.A9 H645 2002
 618.92'8982--dc21   2002027533

ISBN 1 84310 741 4

Printed and Bound in Great Britain by
Athenaeum Press, Gateshead, Tyne and Wear

To my sweet husband
for giving me a family

Contents

1.	About Us	9
2.	About this Book	10
3.	In the Beginning	13
4.	Family Life with Billy	18
5.	Tantrums	24
6.	A Good Day with a Three-Year-Old	26
7.	A Cross-Country Move	31
8.	How We Learned that Billy is Autistic	33
9.	Seeing Autism – and Recognizing What You See	37
10.	Enlightenment Check	41
11.	Coming to Terms	42
12.	A Brief History of One Boy's Autism	45
13.	A Guardian Angel	58
14.	My First Step in Managing Billy – "Buying Time"	61
15.	Rituals	66
16.	Schedules	77
17.	Communicating in Poetry	83
18.	ChOT (The "Choice-Offering Tool")	86
19.	Dealing with Physical Sensitivities	94
20.	Reserves of Body and Soul	100
21.	Starting the Day	103

22.	Organizing the Struggle	107
23.	The Warrior-Parent	111
24.	An Example of a Battle-Plan	114
25.	Another Battle Considered	117
26.	Some Battles in Progress	120
27.	Autism and the Phases of the Moon	123
28.	OMAFED	133
29.	Using OMAFED	135
30.	A Tantrum is not Wrongdoing	138
31.	OMAFED and the Rest of the World	141
32.	Happiness Training	143
33.	Don't Say Don't	149
34.	"We Use Words and Poems and Songs"	152
35.	The Value of Friendship	155
36.	Sibling Shame	160
37.	Books, Books, Books	165
38.	Menu, Please	168
39.	Well-Meaning People	175
40.	A Special Education	181
41.	Summer School	185
42.	The Academy – and Home at Last	189
43.	Epilogue: The Four Stages of Life	192

APPENDIX: BILLY'S WORDS AT AGE FOUR   196

About Us

There are four of us. I am Olga, the mother. The father is Bill.
Francesca, who is ten, is the Big Sister. And Billy – that is
B-I-L-L-Y – is eight years of age. He is officially autistic.

About this Book

Billy was born when Francesca was almost two.

Francesca, a beautiful and well-behaved child, had been a continuous reminder of just how good a mother I was. I felt it was due to my excellent mothering that I had such an admirable child.

When Francesca was a baby, we were living in New York City, on Roosevelt Island, a long, narrow island in the East River right across from mid-town Manhattan. On nice mornings I'd take her to one of the playgrounds on the Island, where I'd meet with other mothers with young children. While Francesca played with the other children in the sand box, I'd drink a cup of coffee and have a pleasant chat with friends.

Mary, one of the mothers, had a son, Brian, only three months older than Francesca. Mary didn't sit on the bench. She didn't drink coffee. She didn't have many chances to chat. Her boy didn't play in the sand box. He was on the run all the time. All Mary had time to do was keep up with him, which wasn't easy.

At that time it never crossed my mind that one day, like Mary, I would be running after *my* boy all over a playground. I thought that if I had more children, they'd all be like Francesca – full of smiles and sweet reason.

Man proposes, God disposes.

Billy was born the very week that we moved from Roosevelt Island to suburban Connecticut. I don't think he planned his appearance to cause maximum confusion; but that was the effect.

Billy was as beautiful a child as Francesca, but as time went on it became clear that his way of interacting with the world around him was not going to earn him a passing grade under any of the usual standards. And, with admirable consistency, I blamed myself for his shortcomings, just as I had credited myself for Francesca's virtues. I thought I had done something right with the girl and I hadn't done quite everything right with the boy – maybe even something wrong! But no matter how deeply I thought about the situation, I never could figure out just what exactly were those "rights" and "wrongs."

There are books on ethics – the "rights" and "wrongs" of moral choices. There are books on etiquette – the "rights" and "wrongs" of social behavior. There are "rights" and "wrongs" for dress codes, for political correctness, for approaching a woman...

There are no clear standards of parenthood. Everyone is left to judge for himself/herself how good a parent he or she is. And when a parent strives to be the best of the best of the best, but things are as bad as they could be (or so it seems), who's to blame? If, like me, you hesitate to blame God, all that's left is to blame yourself. That's a hard lot to live with.

Billy is eight now. We've had eight years of ups and downs, of "rights" and "wrongs." Looking back, I'm now able to sort out at least some things, to sort out in part what actually should be blamed on God and what is to be blamed on us, his parents.

From the top of this eight-year mountain, what we see is that God's will is a work in progress, and our own will is a ticket to help Him in His work.

Most of the frustration in raising an autistic child comes at the moments of hopelessness. When it feels as if nothing can be done.

When Fate seems overwhelming and unmerciful. The burden of raising a special child became easier when we acknowledged that there was a job for us as well, an important and valuable job. Life became lighter when we realized that we could make a difference.

With this book I will try to bring Hope into your house too. This book is for the parent who feels frustrated and helpless under the weight of Fate. Fate may seem overwhelming, but it *can* be invited to step aside and make some room so that the parents may step in and, gently and firmly, bit by bit, take charge.

3

In the Beginning

Billy was born with a worried look on his face, and for the first six months of his life, that look rarely left him. He was a good baby. He was sweet and lovely, with eyes so dark and clear that when you looked at them you knew that you were looking at perfection itself.

He just didn't smile. Tickling and baby talk that would have been enough to bring smiles to twenty babies like Francesca could not drive the worry from Billy's little face. Then, at six months, he finally started rewarding us once in while with a sudden, reserved smile. I used to joke that it took Billy six months to be sure he'd got the right parents.

Billy was about seven months old before I realized just how difficult he was to take care of, in comparison with my daughter. He didn't seem to take much pleasure in life. For Billy, life was struggle.

But I thought, "That's how boys are. Girls come to us good, and boys come to us good and tough; and we've got a tough one. Lots of tough boys become fine gentlemen. Just hang on till you get there."

At that point in my life, I was a tired woman. The babies were less than two years apart, and neither of them was sleeping through the night. They had different schedules in the daytime. It was a time when I was trying to remember how it feels to feel rested, but I couldn't. I didn't have a lot of energy – certainly not enough to stand up to the tornado-like energy which God had generously bestowed upon Billy.

Very early on – about the time he started to smile, actually – it became clear that Billy was going to be a demanding baby. He knew what he wanted, and he was determined to get it at all costs – to himself or anyone else.

For instance: food.

From the beginning, Billy's tastes in food were narrow and rigid; and they weren't necessarily the foods that the child-rearing books recommend.

Francesca, now ten, still drinks soda only on the few occasions when her parents allow it. Billy drank soda starting at eight months old. It wasn't that we wanted him to; but he saw his father drinking soda one evening and wanted a taste – no, demanded a taste – and after that taste, his life was not complete without soda, and soda on a regular basis.

As in eating, so with the rest of Billy's life: he knew what he wanted and insisted on having it – and insisted with such unrelenting and passionate determination that in the end we often gave up just to have some peace in the house. His determination to have whatever pleased his fancy drove us to distraction and at the same time left us in awe. It was amazing to see such force of spirit in such a little body.

It was the same with everything – whatever he saw, he wanted to work his will on.

He demanded to watch television. Francesca never had. Before he could walk, he demanded to be moved from one place to another. Francesca at that age was content to sit in one place for long periods. He insisted on playing with things that weren't toys – Dad's tools, kitchen utensils, anything he could or couldn't reach. Francesca religiously treated only toys as subjects of her will.

He also resisted any change from one event to another. We assumed at the time that he was resisting giving up whatever he was happily doing. Only later did we realize that he was resisting change itself. Only later did we come to understand the force of the word "transition" – an important word to the parent of any autistic child, a word as important as "tantrum" – another word we never thought of at that time in relation to our own children and our own lives.

We thought of Billy as a very normal, if very tough, little guy. We started calling Billy "Little Bill" – not after his father, but after the sheriff in the Clint Eastwood movie *Unforgiven*: a tough-as-nails character who knew what he wanted and wouldn't be crossed by anybody.

Our pediatrician, a man of about seventy who had treated children all his life, also saw Billy as a healthy, normal baby with nothing to be concerned about. When Billy was about eighteen months old, I asked the doctor if I should be concerned that Billy wasn't talking. The doctor said, "No. He'll talk. He's just fine."

But Billy wasn't "just fine."

The first person to suggest that our son was not "just fine" was a friend who was visiting from the faraway country of Kazakhstan. Roza, a specialist in children with developmental problems, told us it was troubling that Billy didn't talk. She was convinced that something was wrong and that we should have him checked.

We reacted to Roza's advice in what I call a "duck in the water" sort of way–the words pour over you, but somehow they don't get inside you, as if you're coated with a protective oil. When the words stop, you shake them off, and it's as if you've never heard them.

Roza came back to visit half a year later. Billy was big and healthy, but he still didn't talk. This time, when she advised us to check Billy, she sounded worried. And this time we heard her.

Roza told us about early-intervention programs for children whose development is delayed. She said that these programs had been initiated in the United States and that they had a high success rate. She was trying to find resources to support early-intervention programs in her native Kazakhstan. In her view, we were lucky, with a child with special needs, that we happened to live in the United States.

This time I became convinced that I had to do anything that could be done. We lived in Connecticut then, a state which did in fact have an early-intervention program. I contacted the program. A team of three people – a psychologist, a speech therapist and an occupational therapist – came to our house to evaluate Billy. The verdict was "speech delay plus behavioral problems." Therapy was prescribed, to be administered once a week, in the form of a forty-five-minute combination of speech therapy and occupational therapy. We followed the prescription. But it didn't change Billy.

In the Russian language there is an expression "like putting a poultice on a corpse" – a way to describe a well-intentioned waste of time. That's how I felt about Billy's weekly therapy. But I didn't know what else there was to do.

A year later, in 1996, we moved back to New York City. Different state, different services. Another evaluation, quite a bit more elaborate now. Billy was evaluated in Manhattan at a respectable midtown institution with specialists who had PhDs in child psychology. We brought Billy for several appointments. Each time, the professionals spent an average of thirty minutes with the boy, engaging him in games and activities meant to help place him in an appropriate special-education slot. The experts' task was to prepare a description of Billy's deficiencies in order to determine the services he would receive. The description of Billy, this time at the age of three, was, again, "speech delay plus behavioral problems."

Billy was to join a special-education class for about three hours a day, four days a week.

The class was a great help for me. It gave me a break. But, once more, it wasn't much help for Billy.

4

Family Life with Billy

Most people's expectations, when they imagine having a family, are probably pretty similar. Picture a cozy evening in front of a fireplace. The television is showing an engaging family movie. The father is reading a newspaper. The mother is combing her daughter's hair. The son sits on the carpet with his teddy, happily involved with the movie. It's idyllic. When the clock strikes nine, the children kiss the parents and go to bed. The parents wish them "Goodnight, children," and finish the evening enjoying one another's company.

Our evenings by the fire generally took a different course. When we watched an engaging family movie, Billy felt the need to stand right in front of the television. We'd remind him that we can't see through him. He'd sit down, but, like the Energizer bunny, he'd pop up the very next moment and place himself again in front of the television. We'd ask him again to sit down. Again, he'd sit down, only to get up the very next moment.

Billy had to move all the time. He'd be climbing on his father, who was trying to read the paper. He'd be jumping on the couch, hanging from chairs, dropping books, laughing out loud, screaming and bothering all of us in his creative and persistent way.

With Francesca, I remember magnificent moments of peace. Sometimes these moments came as she napped while I carried her on a long walk. They came as I watched her play around the house with her toys. I'd put pillows around her so she wouldn't fall and hurt herself, I'd give her toys, and she played for a long time and made happy baby sounds. I took lots of pictures.

With Billy, the only moments of peace were the ones when he was asleep. That's why I rocked him to sleep in my arms for as long as I could comfortably hold him – just to feel his body calm, to see his lashes falling gently onto his cheeks.

Francesca did not scream the moment she awoke. Billy did. Whenever Billy woke, I had to run to the rescue. I was on the run all day long. There were no moments of peace. He might need a toy which was too far to reach, or he might want an object which he couldn't be allowed to have. He seemed to have an endless need for something, whether it was a drink, or a snack, or to go outside. He never stopped insisting on his own agenda.

At some point I realized that not only were there no quiet, relaxed moments with Billy; I was not able to start and finish any chore without being endlessly interrupted to attend to his demands.

My notion of life's pleasures changed at that point. I started wishing for a lovely quiet time washing dishes, just me, singing a song, and the dishes. Or I'd wish for an evening of uninterrupted ironing, smoothing the wrinkles on fabrics and becoming one with the iron.

Public appearances with baby Francesca were sheer delight. She loved going places, and she loved smiling at people. That, combined with the fact that she was the cutest little girl (of course), brought us many admiring comments. Bill and I loved taking little Francesca with us for walks to nice restaurants in Manhattan. Dressed like a princess, she'd sit in a high chair and play sweetly throughout our meal.

Billy did not sit in a high chair in a restaurant – not for longer than three minutes. After three minutes, we had to take him out of the chair; otherwise he'd have jumped out by himself. Trying to keep him in the chair was not a good idea, because to any restraint he responded with indignation, violent and loud enough to cure that intention immediately.

Once out of the chair, Billy had to play with the silverware, with the glasses, with the napkins. He'd have to venture around the restaurant exploring new territory. He'd take an interest in the belongings of people at other tables. Our dining experience would be reduced to taking turns protecting the house from Billy. We took Billy out for dinner with us exactly two times before he was three. Both times were to a Chinese place on 38th Street where we were long-time clients. The owner knew us before we had children. He was delighted when we brought Francesca with us. He was very generous in his acceptance of Billy. But other than those two times, we didn't go out with Billy to places where food was served to seated people. McDonald's was the place for us, a place which could provide french fries quick, and where a misbehaving child could be got out the door with minimal loss of dignity.

With Francesca there was never a problem in finding a babysitter or a nursery school. She was a delight to have around, she was good to other children, and she loved to play with children of any ages.

I couldn't find any long-term help with Billy. When we lived in Connecticut, we had a big house, and I hired a live-in Russian nanny. After we met to try one another out and to give her a chance to meet Billy, we made a six-month commitment to each other. We both hoped for a great experience.

For the first month, I tried to train her to do a job that demanded permanent watchfulness, tremendous tolerance and acceptance and readiness to stretch one's boundaries to new limits. That is, I tried to train her to take care of Billy. She couldn't do it. So I gave up training her and took care of Billy myself. This made her feel bad, which, combined with homesickness, brought her to depression. Her experience was one of surviving several months in a strange country in a house with an unruly child. My experience was one of taking care of a depressed Russian woman as well as my children. And I didn't dare repeat it.

But I did long for a break, even for an hour or two. Francesca was then going several hours a week to a home-based nursery run by a lovely American woman, Nancy. I asked Nancy if she would take Billy.

Nancy knew that I was tired, and she really wanted to help me. She tried to have Billy for two hours. But he wandered away from the play area. He broke the dividing gate between the play area and the living room. He took toys away from other children.

When I came to pick him up, Nancy said, "Sorry, Olga, I can't do it."

Between the ages of two and four, Billy was expelled from seven nursery schools. People were always willing to give him a try. When signing him in, I invariably warned a new place that my boy had behavioral problems. The invariable response was, "Oh, no problem. We've had children with behavioral problems. We're very good with them!" – only to change, one or two days later, to "Sorry, we can't handle Billy."

But I have to bring some light into this dark picture which I've painted for you. We had one good experience.

You may ask me, since I knew what my son was like, why did I try to sign him up anywhere at all?

The reason was this: I believed that if among Billy's caretakers there happened to be a person who could become his soulmate, then he would be all right.

I could manage him myself much better than any of the people at the places he was expelled from. At each place there were incidents which I knew could have been easily prevented if only there was a person who had, in his or her heart, a desire to understand Billy.

Eventually, we found such a person. She worked at an Orthodox Jewish nursery school on East 63rd Street in Manhattan. We didn't know she was there when we enrolled Billy, though.

We had signed Billy up for several afternoon hours and held our breath. We basically expected that he would be home again within a day or two, expelled for misbehavior. But it didn't happen the first day. It didn't happen the second day either. Nor the third, fourth, or fifth. After a few weeks, Billy was still going to the school, and we realized that he was doing fine! Billy loved the school. He loved the games. He loved the music time, even though the songs were all in Hebrew, and all he'd ever heard was English and Russian.

And then, one afternoon, after Billy had been there for two months, we were asked not to bring him back in the morning.

Sarah, one of his teachers, had gone to Israel on vacation. Nobody else could handle Billy. Sarah was his soulmate at that place.

I saw her again later, after she came back. She told me she missed Billy and felt bad about losing him. "If I'd been there, they would have kept him," she said. "I liked him. His ways didn't irritate me. I thought he was interesting. And he's a good kid."

Billy had to climb to the top of any structure he encountered. He was without fear and without judgment. If there was a fence, he had to climb it. If there was a playhouse, he had to get onto its roof. At one playground we frequented, there was a long narrow beam high in the air between two playground structures. He loved to walk it from one end to the other. I spent hours walking below him, ready to catch him when he fell; but he never did. He loved a slide, as long as it was a dramatic one. The higher the better. And every time he'd get to the bottom of the slide, he'd sit a moment to pull his pants legs down to cover the space that had opened between his socks and his pants as he came down the slide.

When Billy moved, he ran. When Billy ran, he did not notice other children in his way. He treated them like obstacles to be brushed aside, whether they happened to be on the ground or on the top level of a playground tower. So I had to keep after him all the time. He could harm another child without knowing it.

If something at the playground caught Billy's fancy for a moment, but it was already taken by another child, he'd try to let the other child know that he wanted to take a turn at it. But, since he didn't know how to express himself in words, the way he expressed his desire was to push, and if that didn't work, to bite or hit. He could react with the quickness of a wild animal, so I had to be close to him at all times, ready to resolve any problem. If it happened that I wasn't sufficiently alert, I usually regretted it. Trouble was bound to happen.

I hated it when Billy was aggressive toward another child. The child cried, and I felt sorry for the child. I wished I could give that child some comfort and some kind words, but all my attention had to be given to Billy, to tamp down his emotions to prevent a tantrum. I'd offer my apologies to the mother of the other child, who would look at me scornfully and often chastise me for not controlling my boy.

Tantrums

When Billy was upset about something, he had a tantrum.

We had heard the word "tantrum" before we had Billy, of course; but I'm not sure whether Bill or I had ever actually seen one. Certainly not with Francesca.

People with typical children talk about their child throwing a tantrum; but I'm not sure that most of them have ever seen a real tantrum either.

A Billy tantrum started with the boy whining and insisting on getting his way. And if he didn't get his way, the protest followed immediately. There were tears. Then there were more tears, building and building to a hysterical degree. The next stage was rage. At this stage Billy would easily become aggressive. He wasn't attacking us, but he was responding in an aggressive way to our attempts to calm him down. If we offered him a hug, he'd push us away. If we tried to give him a toy, he'd throw it down. He'd kick. He'd lie on the floor and arch his back so that only his head and feet were on the floor. His face would get so red it was frightening. Then he'd start choking on his tears and on the stuff running from his nose. At the peak of a tantrum, his face would become swollen, he'd be sweating all over, trembling, having hiccups, and his whole body would twitch.

Billy's tantrums became worse as he approached his third birthday. He got bigger and stronger. It was no longer possible just to grab his little body and stick him in the stroller or the car seat and strap him in.

How did Billy's tantrums affect us?

During a tantrum it felt as if invisible vibrations were piercing us. And as the tantrum escalated, those vibrations became more and more piercing. We were victims of Billy's tantrums just as much as he was, or maybe even more. We couldn't escape those vibrations; they penetrated us and threw us as far off balance as Billy was.

We knew of only three ways, at that time, to get Billy out of a tantrum.

1. We give in. Billy gets what he wants.

2. Something diverts his attention.

3. We all endure until he drifts into miserable, tear-stained, exhausted sleep.

Most of the time we opted for number one. Number two required a substantial offering – something like a trip to McDonald's. Number three was too hard on all of us.

A Good Day with a Three-Year-Old

When Billy was three, we moved back from Connecticut to Roosevelt Island in New York City. Here's an example of a fairly typical day with Billy after the move. It's by far not the worst of our days from that time.

7:00 a.m. – temper tantrum #1

It's time to get up. Billy refuses to leave the comfort of his bed. We struggle. I use a combination of sweet words and firm persuasion.

We struggle through washing, dressing and breakfast.

7:45 a.m. – temper tantrum #2

Billy refuses to put on his winter clothes – coat, hat, mittens. We struggle.

Then we finally have a good moment in the morning – the ride in the elevator from the 16th floor to the lobby. Billy likes that. I just have to be sure to use my back as a shield to protect the elevator buttons. Otherwise we'll spend a chunk of time riding up and down.

8:05 a.m. – temper tantrum #3

Billy refuses to leave the building. He does not care to be immersed in the cool Atlantic breeze of a New York autumn morning.

This temper tantrum could be a long one. If the weather is chilly and windy, Billy will struggle all the way to the bus stop and until the bus comes.

When the bus does come, we have a temporary shift in Billy energy. He is excited to get into the bus. He knows that, inside, the bus is warm, and he is eager to sit in the back row of seats. Behind the back row of seats there is a wide shelf over the engine, where, if the bus is not too full, Billy can have some freedom to jump and climb. But often the seats in the back are taken, and then we have to endure that most unpleasant thing – a public temper tantrum.

8:20 a.m. – temper tantrum #4

The seats in the back are taken. We struggle.

Temper tantrums on public transportation are the worst of public temper tantrums, because you really want to get somewhere, and if you get off the bus, there's just going to be another temper tantrum because you got off the bus. So you stay, enduring not only the boy's wrath but also the public's. The public's wrath is based on their certainty that you know nothing about raising a child. (In New York City, people often take a crying child as a personal insult.)

We get out at the tram station. The tram ride, which gets us from Roosevelt Island over the East River to Manhattan, is usually bearable, sometimes even pleasant. I hold Billy in my arms so that he can see down through the windows. Billy likes the view. The busyness of the Manhattan scene is like science fiction, with helicopters, the constant rage of ambulances and fire engines, the boats and barges on the East River going upstream or down toward the Statue of Liberty.

Billy likes the view. But that does not mean that I can relax and enjoy the view with him. Billy's ability to spot a chance for trouble and get into it is much sharper than my ability to prevent it from happening. I'm at the peak of my awareness.

From the tram we walk five blocks to Billy's school. This little trip is hard too. Billy has little sense of danger and no sense of fear. As for Manhattan streets with their erratic traffic, he considers them a perfect place for a small boy to run free. Five blocks to the school, an endless adventure for him, seems an endless journey to me.

We are lucky that Billy likes the school and doesn't mind being left there. His three hours in the school, from 8:30 to 11:30 am, are my big break.

12:00 p.m. – temper tantrum #5

This one is, again, on the bus. I should have expected this one; but I didn't. I never did, at that time of our lives. Looking back, I can see that many of Billy's temper tantrums were predictable. They occurred again and again in the same environments. What later changed was our ability to predict them and either avoid them or cope.

12:30 p.m. – temper tantrum #6

We're home. Billy wants soda. I refuse to let him have it.

1:00 p.m. – temper tantrum #7

Billy refuses to take a nap. I force him to take one, using a combination of reading, massage, lullabies and plain persuasion. It takes at least half an hour to put him to sleep. But when his eye-lashes finally drop on his cheeks, I step into a different reality – the sense of having a peaceful home. He will let me spend not much more than an hour in that peace. I use the time to catch up with the house. (It took me a long time to come to understand that I should have used the time only to regenerate my nerve cells.)

3:00 p.m. – temper tantrum #8

We need to bring Francesca from her school. Billy protests at having to put on his winter clothes yet again.

3:25 p.m. – temper tantrum #9

At the school, Billy wants to play with things in Francesca's classroom. It is not permitted.

3:45 p.m. – temper tantrum #10

We step into the grocery store. Billy wants to run loose. I make him sit strapped in the stroller. He dislikes it very loudly.

4:15 p.m. – temper tantrum #11

We are at the playground. Billy is interested in a swing that is already occupied by another child. Tragedy.

5:00 p.m. – temper tantrum #12

Billy wants to climb out onto the narrow edge of a 10-foot wall. I try to stop him. He doesn't give up. So I give up, take both children and go home.

5:25 p.m. – temper tantrum #13

Billy wants to watch television. This would be acceptable to me in principle; but in practice Francesca has to do her homework, and we need to wait until she is done.

6:45 p.m. – temper tantrum #14

Billy wants to watch television right after dinner. I insist that he have a bath first.

7:00 p.m. – temper tantrum #15

We are in the bathroom. Billy rebels against having to take off his clothes and get into the water. Against anguished resistance I undress him, make him use the potty and get him into the tub. As always, after about five minutes of sitting in warm, comfortable water, a shift takes place. Billy starts enjoying his bath.

7:45 p.m. – temper tantrum #16

Billy refuses to get out of the bath. I have to drain the water and endure his indignation.

Usually that's about the last severe tantrum of the day.

The time between Billy's tantrums was not necessarily a peaceful time of relaxed interaction between parent and child. That state of affairs was practically nonexistent, for in the time between tantrums the boy required help to recover from the tantrum that had just ended, and this recovery in itself was an emotionally demanding affair. And no matter how we tried to prevent it from happening, at the end of one tantrum the boy's brain started to become agitated again, making him ready for a full blow during the following tantrum. The tantrums wore on everyone around him. Trying to soothe his agitation was like trying to stop him from sliding into a swamp, only to be swallowed by the swamp along with him.

Only much later did we learn to resist this overwhelming power that dragged Billy and us into the swamp, to keep Billy from sliding in and to keep ourselves from sliding with him. These days, we notice that he is sliding as soon as his toes touch the mud of negative emotions. Maybe we'll lose him until he's up to his knees or to his thighs; but we haven't lost him over his head or even to his heart for more than two years now.

We haven't forgotten how it was before. Without that past, we'd not be counting so many blessings today.

A Cross-Country Move

In 1997 we decided to move from New York City.

Bill and I had reasons of our own; but Billy was a reason too. We had realized that taking care of our boy in winter was much harder than during warm weather. He reacted painfully to cold, to wind, to snow. Going outside was not an appealing option for a good part of the New York winter. Staying inside was a chore as well, with a boy upon whom God had bestowed energy sufficient to destroy the Roman Empire. I wished to be able to keep whatever was left of my sanity. California was Hope.

We drove across the country. The trip was not as hard as we anticipated. If the world was moving around him, Billy was generally satisfied. When we stopped in Nebraska to visit relatives, he adopted our car as home and spent a lot of time sitting in it. He preferred that to being in new places with new people.

House-hunting with Billy was hard. He made every new experience a test of the emotional limits of everyone around him. I tried to find a preschool that would accept him while we hunted. I explained to the administrators that in New York he had been diagnosed as a child with "behavioral problems and speech delay."

Two places agreed to take Billy.

The first one lasted three days. Something about the place offended Billy. On the third day he pooped at the top of the playground slide. We were asked not to bring him back.

The second place lasted a little longer. But Billy was not good at following rules he disagreed with, and he sometimes expressed his disagreement by biting people. One day he bit a fellow preschooler, whose parents, enraged, threatened to take the school to court. When we came to take Billy home that day, we were asked not to bring him back.

But even those few days without children helped us. We rushed around town checking out places for rent.

One lucky morning an ad in the paper led us to a house in the central San Diego district of Mission Hills. The house overlooked a canyon abundant with vegetation, birds, skunks and even foxes. It also had a longer view – from the second floor we could see the city's airport, with planes, like mighty birds, landing and taking off; and beyond the airport we could see the ocean and, in clear weather, islands far away, off the coast of Mexico.

We rented the place. We brought our things from storage and went about settling in. Our address placed us in the San Diego Unified School District. It was mid-August, and it was time to find schools for our children.

Francesca was easy. The local elementary school, a few blocks from our house, had a very good reputation. We enrolled our daughter in first grade, with a teacher who loved teaching. Francesca had a whole year of good days, met her best friend ever and received many awards.

We knew that placing the boy would be harder. We started investigating private preschools; but before we found one, Fate intervened in the form of a well-dressed woman.

How We Learned that Billy is Autistic

That August of 1997, four years after the birth of our son, I finally put one and two together. These were my revelations:

1. Billy's behavior (like the morning fog) = Not My Fault.

2. Continuing the job of full-time mom to Billy and nothing else = Not A Good Idea.

The first conclusion came with the realization that I had overdone both my pride in my excellence at raising Francesca and my guilt at failing to make a proper boy out of Billy. I decided that I needed to let go of some of my expectations for my children, to take one day at a time, and to be happy for any progress they might make, whether or not it was progress by conventional standards.

The second conclusion came with the realization that I had been underestimating how tired I was. In fact I was worn out, physically and emotionally. I had to admit that, since Billy was born, I had become less happy, more irritable, less tolerant, more agitated, less creative, and more tearful.

1 + 2 = I needed to do something else, besides taking care of Billy. (And his sister, of course; but that was nothing.)

The state of mind that I was in would easily have qualified me for therapy. I opted for something else. I signed up for a course in fashion design at the Fashion Careers College of San Diego.

It proved to be a wise decision. I got to spend time away from home, in a very creative environment, among young people for whom anything relating to children was boring, to say the least. For thirty hours each week I immersed myself in an environment that made it easy to forget about the stresses of home. I was creating designs, drawing, sewing, talking about fashion and working with fabrics – things I had always loved. It was the best therapy possible.

But my design course had another benefit, an unexpected one. At my admission interview, I told the director of admissions that I might have to miss some classes because I had a child who might often need my support at home. The director of admissions was a blonde young woman, heavily jeweled, with pronounced and skillful makeup, clothed in layers and color combinations that were very appropriate for a fashion design school.

She asked me to tell her more about Billy. Now, that was a test for my patience. It was not easy for me to talk about Billy's problems, not even with professional educators or psychologists. It seemed foolish to talk about him just to support the idle curiosity of a fashion-design college administrator. But I wanted to be polite, so I told her a little about Billy – that he had problems with transitions, that he had frequent temper tantrums, that he didn't talk but constantly made repetitive noises. Most of all, that he was wonderfully lovely and likable but surely a handful.

"He's autistic," said the director of admissions.

I bristled. "What? Why do you say that?" I demanded.

My only acquaintance with the word "autism" until then came from the film *Rain Man*. Billy was not like the autistic man in the movie. Not at all. There was no way he could be autistic. What did she know, anyway?

"Several years ago I had a boyfriend," she said, "whose daughter was just like your son. We broke up, but here's his phone number. Just don't tell him that I gave it to you."

I was sure she didn't know what she was talking about. Yet as soon as I got home I called her ex-boyfriend. There was no answer, but I left a message on his answering machine. Since I couldn't let him know how I'd got his number, my message was a little vague.

He didn't call back.

I left another message, and then another.

He called a few days later. He said, "My girlfriend says a woman with an accent keeps leaving messages for me. Is that you?"

I admitted that it was.

He sounded annoyed. Feeling a little lost, and with my Russian accent more pronounced than usual, I tried to explain why I had called him.

But the moment he understood what I was calling about, that I was a mother of a child who needed help, his attitude changed entirely. He no longer cared who had given me his number. We talked for an hour. He told me about his daughter, and the more he said the more lost I felt. Lost, but found.

All of Billy's strange habits, all his unique ways, were unique no longer. I was hearing the story of a little girl who fought against transitions, who had numberless temper tantrums, who barked like a dog for hours on end after each time she watched the video *101 Dalmatians*, and who rolled on the floor each time she watched a video about a seal. Everything her father told me about her sounded like Billy. And her father was telling me that she was autistic.

He gave me the name of a psychologist, an expert in autism, whom we could see in San Diego.

We took Billy to the psychologist. And we walked out of his office knowing that our son was autistic.

It is hard to learn that your child is autistic. But it is so much easier to know than not to know.

9

Seeing Autism – and Recognizing What You See

Four years have passed since we learned our boy is autistic. In that time my husband and I have met at least four children who, to us, were obviously autistic, but whose parents had no idea of it.

Once at a playground I met a young mother with two boys. The younger one was in a corner of the sand box, playing with a toy car all by himself. He looked to be about two. He didn't talk. He avoided eye contact and didn't respond to his name. His mother told me with amusement how the boy would play with cars for hours on end but would not accept any other toys, and how he would look endlessly at picture books or watch videos, as long as they were about cars.

She reminded me of myself at the time when I was sure of Billy's uniqueness. Unlike my director of admissions, I was careful not to tell her, "Your boy is autistic," because I was afraid I might frighten her away from getting help. But I tried to send her in that direction more gently, by telling her that he might qualify for free speech therapy. I told her how to go about finding an early-intervention program. I never met her after that, so I don't know if she followed up on my suggestion.

But there was another mother I met at a birthday party for the child of a mutual friend. She was there with her young son, also about two years old; and her boy also reminded me a lot of Billy.

He had Billy's tendency to avoid eye contact, to persist with amazing intensity in doing one thing for a long time. He walked along the walls of the room making putt-putt noises. He didn't speak.

This mother followed my suggestion to seek early intervention. At the first evaluation meeting she was informed that her son was autistic. She called our friend in tears. But help for her boy started when he was only two years old, and his progress was marvelous. I wish we had known about Billy's autism when he was two and not four, for the older an autistic child grows, the less are the chances for drastic improvement.

But yet...

But yet, Billy had been evaluated by all those early-intervention specialists in Connecticut and New York, and if any of them suspected he was autistic, they didn't even whisper it to us – even though, as we now know, Billy was the very picture of autism.

Two years were lost, years of great importance in starting therapy. Real therapy, not just a "poultice for a corpse."

But at two, to the specialists, he had been just a difficult boy who didn't talk. His vocabulary was three or four words; but those few words gave us – and his pediatrician, and even the early- intervention specialists – confidence that in fact he *could* speak, and that "one of these days" he would start talking in full sentences.

I remember a Russian joke about a little boy who didn't talk. One day, when he was about five, he looked at his mother and said in perfect Russian, "Mother, this tea isn't hot."

The mother was astonished. "You know how to speak! Why didn't you speak before?"

"Before, the tea was always hot."

I must have been catering to Billy's needs perfectly, because Billy didn't find a good reason to speak for a long time.

Many autistic children display few obviously odd behaviors at early age. They may look quite normal to an unaccustomed eye. Therapists who have no specific training in working with autistic children may not recognize one – as we learned. Yet an adult who has spent months and years with an autistic child learns to recognize the intensity, the seeming aloofness and the disguised anxiety of a child who can't find a comfortable place for himself in this world. We know one when we see one.

Autism may manifest itself in a variety of forms and with differing severity. The most common manifestations are delayed speech, poor eye contact, low tolerance for transitions, frequent temper tantrums, rigid and limited taste in foods, patterns of repetitive movements and noises, and fixation on one activity or interest (one child may play only with toy cars, another with airplanes; Billy's fixation is dragons–dragon books, dragon stories, dragon words, dragon toys, dragon videos...). The depth of any of these manifestations varies greatly from child to child. While one child may not speak at all, another may utter a few words, while others speak fluently. One child may be happy, another depressed; one may be aggressive, another mild and sweet-tempered. Nine out of ten are boys. And they are often unusually handsome.

Soon after we received Billy's diagnosis, I was in that stage that parents of autistic children go through soon after diagnosis, calling anyone and everyone I could find who might be able to tell me more about my boy's condition. I telephoned a woman expert in Arizona whose name someone had given me, a woman of great experience and patience in dealing with autistic children and their parents. I remember most the question she asked me near the end of our conversation: "By the way, this may seem a strange question, but...is your boy unusually handsome?"

"Why...yes," I said.

"They often are," she said. "Although nobody knows quite why."

And he is.

But I thought I knew why – because he is my son.

Enlightenment Check

Some time ago I came up with an idea for a new business.

"One Day Enlightenment Check!
Fast and Certain!
In only one day you will learn whether you have attained
Buddhahood!
Accurate results guaranteed!"

A customer would be allowed to spend one day alone with Billy. Payment would be made in advance, and there would be no refund for early return of Billy. The return of Billy before the end of the day means that the client still has work to do before achieving Enlightenment.

Coming to Terms

There is a conventional understanding about what makes up a "good" child.

A good child listens to his/her parents; is quiet most of the time, especially in public places; asks for permission before touching anything; and eats, reads, does his/her work, plays and goes to bed at times set by the adults.

A child is "bad" when the child is noisy, hits or bites other children, is out of control, or does not obey.

Notice that the paragraph about "good" children uses the conjunction "and," while the one about bad children uses the conjunction "or." It takes a lot of things to make a "good" child, but only one to make a "bad" one.

The making of good and bad children may vary slightly from one culture or religion to another – but only slightly.

I was raised in a Moldavian town in the southern part of the Soviet Union. My husband was raised in a tiny village in Nebraska, out there in the middle of the prairie. More than ten thousand miles lie between the places where we were brought up. We spoke different languages, we were taught to honor different Gods, and we listened to different winds.

Yet the understanding of what makes a child "good" which we brought with us from our disparate childhoods is astonishingly similar. And Billy did not fit that understanding.

One of the hardest things in raising an autistic child is to be able to free oneself from conventional judgment about your child's behavior.

Conventionally we praise a child when the child is "good" and encourage the "good" traits. A "good" child makes us happy and content.

Conventionally we scold or punish a child when the child is "bad" and discourage the "bad" traits. A "bad" child makes us unhappy and sad – as well as irritated, upset, and prone to ignoble displays of emotion.

The conventional standards are clear.

But it's not so clear how to apply them to an autistic child, whose brain does not necessarily recognize the judgments of what is "acceptable" that seem to be built into most of us.

Where do we draw the line between what is "acceptable" and what is not? And how do we put those judgment lines in the right place for a child who lacks judgment?

My conclusion is that for the parent of an autistic child, the lines are in permanent motion, their positions shifting constantly, fitting no pattern. A line is where we allow it to be at a certain moment, and its position is guided by how great our emotional strength is.

If Billy breaks a memento that is dear to our hearts, we might take it philosophically one day: "It was time for the thing to die!" Another day we might be desperately beyond the reach of any philosophy.

Billy is eight now, and many things have changed over the past few years. One thing has remained permanent: we can never predict where we would place our judgment lines on any given day, whether far in the future or as near as tomorrow.

I know we are doing better. Overall, our combined emotional strength is more powerful in the year 2002 than it was in the year

1997. Or 1998. Or 1999, or 2000, or 2001. Overall, we've gained more wisdom and balance in drawing the judgment lines.

That is overall. It does not mean that at any specific moment on a lovely morrow my reaction to yet another trick of Billy's will be calm and wise. It may happen that I will display ignoble emotions, Ladies and Gentlemen. It may.

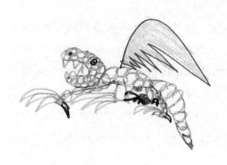

A Brief History of One Boy's Autism

Billy is eight now. His symptoms of autism have changed continuously. Here's how he has developed since age two, when it first began to seem that things were not quite right. (Ever since he started preschool at age four, his schooling has been a big part of his development; but I will only mention it here, and discuss it in detail later, in chapters 40–42.)

At two

Billy doesn't speak more than a few isolated words. He is fascinated with trains, and his first word is *poyezd*, the Russian word for train. Whenever he sees one, he says "*poyezd!*" repeatedly and enthusiastically (if quite inaccurately – it's a hard word even for an adult English-speaker).

He avoids eye contact.

He is very attached to his soft stuffed bunny. He will not go to bed without it. Some evenings we end up crawling all over the house until we find it.

Other toys don't bring much happiness to him.

He is eternally restless, in need of something new. Except for one thing…

The only thing that captures his attention for long is the sight of men at work. Out kitchen is being remodeled, and Billy loves to watch the carpenters, the plumber, the electrician, the painters… He will watch them for hours.

He is very attached to television. He watches public-television children's shows for two or three hours a day. Every time we turn off the set, he has a temper tantrum.

He is not able to play with other children, including his sister.

He is very rigid in his choice of foods. He eats Cheerios but no other cereal. He will eat a peanut-butter-and-jelly sandwich, some baby foods, cake when he can get it. He drinks apple juice, and soda when he can get it. Until about the time of his first birthday, he drank milk, but then he stopped.

Potty training is not worth the attempt.

He has temper tantrums throughout the day. We can explain some of them. We are bewildered by others. For example, every time I try to strap him into his car seat, he screams and arches his back, thrusting out his chest and stomach. This is a real struggle for me, for he is big and strong for his age. Since our suburban life is so dependent on car travel, this struggle takes a lot of my energy. One day, after a painful strapping experience, as I'm watching my boy and wondering what on earth can be done to keep him from having these car-seat tantrums, I notice that he is trying hard to bend over and, apparently, to pull down his pants legs. I realize that as he sits in his car seat, his pants legs are pulled up and a thin strip of skin is exposed between his pants and his socks. And I see that he is trying very hard to cover that strip of skin. I help him. I pull his pants legs down. To my surprise, the boy immediately stops crying. His tantrum ceases. He can't talk, but he looks at me with grateful eyes.

And I remember then what he has always done on the slide in the park. He loves the slide; but each time he comes down, at the bottom before he stands up, he carefully pulls down his pants legs, first one and then the other.

At three

Billy uses about ten words.

He makes practically no eye contact.

He is still very attached to his bunny.

He is intensely interested in exploring any new environment, but he recognizes no authority. This combination makes it practically impossible to visit other people's houses. We experiment a little but, after reimbursing a neighbor $120 for a lamp that Billy pushed to the floor, we cease taking chances. We felt good that no one was hurt.

He is not capable of playing with other children, although it is obvious that he enjoys being around them. On playgrounds and in playrooms Billy becomes the cause of frequent conflicts because he will not tolerate other children "invading his space." He is unwilling to share. He cannot be coaxed to share. He cannot be forced to share. He cannot be *forced* to do anything. We are convinced he would die first. Death before submission.

Billy is more and more attached to television. He starts to impersonate and relive the stories that he watches. A story about a train will make him "choo-choo" for hours; a story about dogs will make him bark for hours.

However, he starts learning to look at picture books, and he likes to be read to – as long as the reading is very theatrical and animated.

He loves to play in water. Any kind of water – his bath, puddles, the ocean.

He walks to the refrigerator and points to the food that he wants, but he still has very limited tastes and will eat nothing not to his taste. He discovers McDonald's and adds french fries to his menu.

Potty training is attempted. It is not successful.

At four

Billy's eye contact has deteriorated steadily since he was six months old. Then he could stare into my eyes. At two, he avoided looking me in the eye, and at three he made practically no eye contact. Now, at four, it is clear that, in looking at a person, he prefers to look anywhere but in the eyes.

We've lost his bunny. This is a hard time, until we discover that Billy likes soft cotton balls and that he will go to bed nicely if he gets one to hold in his hand. This is a great discovery, since it is much easier to renew the supply of cotton balls than of favorite bunnies. Cotton balls begin to go everywhere with him.

He starts to chew on his clothes. He also begins to suck his thumb incessantly.

We succeed in getting him to eat hot dogs. Hot dogs become an important addition to french fries and soda. He also develops a taste for chocolate, and he starts searching the refrigerator and the cabinets for goodies. One day when I am home with both children, I realize that I do not hear Billy. The house is quiet. I search all the rooms, run through the closets with no luck. With my heart pounding, I rush around our neighborhood calling his name, to no avail. I tell myself that I will search the house one more time and then call the police. Going through the bedrooms again, I realize that in my bedroom there is something under the covers. Holding my breath, I raise a corner of the bedspread. My little boy is sitting there, his face dark brown, covered with chocolate, and his brown eyes blinking at me out of the darkness. He is holding a container of sticky chocolate muffin mix, made up and ready to go into the muffin cups, which he must have taken from the refrigerator. He has been eating it with his hands. His master plan obviously was to get down as much of the mix as he could; and he succeeded at it. And even though the boy and all my sheets are covered with chocolate, all I can feel is just happiness to have found him.

So, we discovered a little slyness in Billy. (It would prove not to be the last time, alas.)

He has become very specific in the toys he likes and dislikes. Knights, dragons, and dinosaurs he likes.

He learns to make his own trips to the bathroom, although he still has accidents; but he doesn't respond to the usual toilet-training maneuvers. Appeals to his pride do not work, and we aren't able to penetrate him with our enthusiasm. Showing him the difference between dirty underwear and clean, and stressing the joys of clean, also doesn't work.

A friend, eager to help, suggests that we should use as an incentive something he really, really wants. What he really, really wants is a knight's outfit – a helmet, a shield, a sword. I haven't encouraged his infatuation with aggressive toys, and I've refused to buy him swords; but one day in a store I find a magnificent set of knight's attire – a helmet, a shield, and a beautiful gold and silver sword, all shining like the sun. The set is in a clear plastic cover, so it can be seen before opening. I take it home and show it to Billy. It takes his breath away, he is so thrilled to see it! I take him to the bathroom. I hang that set high above the door, too high for him to climb to, but where he can see it. I hang it there and I say, "Billy, when you start going potty all the time," and I show him the toilet, "I'm going to get that set down, and you can play with it." In an instant, all the happiness and joy that was in him dissipates. Suddenly I have an indifferent Billy. I try to excite him: "Billy, come on! Isn't it wonderful? All you have to do is go potty to get that set!" But no matter what I say, he is just bland. He leaves the bathroom.

For days afterward, whenever he has an accident, I try to get him to the bathroom. I say, "See that toy? I'd like to give it to you, but I can't. I'm sorry, but you had an accident." But each time he just refuses to look at it, and acts as if it doesn't exist.

I think he has decided that, desirable as the set is, he's not going to be able to earn it; and he would rather not know of it than yearn for it.

The set hangs there for about ten days, until I feel so awful about the whole thing that I give up. One evening I take the set down and take it to the living room and give it to him. He's glad to have it; he opens it and plays with it; but his happiness is nothing to that wonder when he first saw it.

I've never tried buying him again.

His vocabulary is not improving. He's still only at about fifty-five words of active vocabulary. About twenty of those he knows in both English and Russian, and a few only in Russian. (See the Appendix for a list of his words: we made it in preparation to see the autism specialist.) We do not know the extent of his passive vocabulary but we know that he understands much more than he can say. He is not saying "juice," but he knows the word (and he says "sok," which means "juice" in Russian). It's the same with many other words – he knows a lot more than he can say.

Conversely, he tries to use many words that we cannot quite make out.

One day, watching him watch the video of *The Lord of the Rings* (the old Ralph Bakshi animated version), my husband realizes that Billy is speaking the lines just in advance of the action. Moving on through *The Hobbit* and *The Return of the King* (cartoons released in the 1970s by Warner Brothers, telling parts of the tale that Bakshi didn't cover), we find that he has these stories down too, a total of some five hours of drama. We then realize that he has been doing this for a long time, and that he has memorized the dialog of many other videotapes too. It took so long for us to understand what he was doing because his enunciation is so poor.

Temper tantrums are a constant of our life. They are a part of most transitions throughout the day – in or out of bed, in or out of the bath, into or out of the house, into or out of the store…

The psychologist's diagnosis that Billy is autistic opens the way to a lot of help that we had never had before.

The San Diego Regional Center for the Developmentally Disabled provides us with referrals to psychologists, with medical tests and, most important of all, with a home-care aide one night a week so we can go out and relax. (Most teenage babysitters cannot cope with Billy.)

The San Diego Unified School District assigns Billy a spot in a special-education preschool class. We wonder how long he will last there.

And so, at age four, Billy at last meets his guardian angel, Theresa.

Theresa Miles is Billy's preschool teacher, and she becomes his first figure of authority. He stays in her class for the whole year. From her example we learn that it is possible to manage Billy – after all, she does it, even if we don't yet understand quite how. Theresa will have a chapter to herself later in the book. She deserves more than one.

Theresa gets Billy to learn new words. He responds especially to her way of teaching little songs like "Eensy-Beensy Spider." He loves theatrics and animation.

Billy has a very good year in Theresa's classroom. We relax and feel that from now on the San Diego Unified School District will take care of our son's education.

At five

Billy goes on to kindergarten with a new teacher. She is a very nice person, and she tries hard; but she has no training in teaching autistic children. During this school year he causes few problems and learns little.

Without Theresa, Billy again recognizes no authority at school. But he has started to recognize my authority at home, whenever I employ Theresa's tactics.

Billy continues to chew on his clothes. His shirts and jackets are often wet all over the front.

He starts making repetitive noises, something he had never done before.

He also starts making repetitive body movements – spinning in circles, twirling a string in his hand or shaking his head. Sometimes he does several of these things at the same time.

He often becomes a dragon. He walks bent forward, hands clutched in front of him like claws, lower jaw moving down and forward with gnashing teeth, legs bent at the knees, feet stomping. His persistent dragon impersonation intimidates other children.

Potty training is partially successful (he still wears training pants but goes pee-pee on the potty when he is reminded to).

He learns more words. He learns to name colors, numbers and some letters. But, although he can repeat a color name, he cannot identify the color in answer to the question "what color is this?"

He has to be watched whenever he is around other children, because the possibility of an aggressive reaction to something is very high, and it is hard to predict what "something" might be.

As his schedule becomes more structured, we learn to predict what's likely to set off a temper tantrum, and therefore, to some extent (but still not in a structured way, unfortunately), we learn to avoid them.

I master two different ways of controlling his temper tantrums – the techniques I call "buying time" and "OMAFED." (I'll describe these later. See Chapters 14 and 28.)

Billy's menu expands only slightly. He learns to like pizza. Breakfast is a toasted peanut-butter-and-jelly sandwich ("toasters"). Toasters must always be cut into four pieces.

I develop in him a habit of having a night-time snack of apples and carrots and a full cup of apple juice.

At six

Billy goes to first grade. He loves books, discovers computer games. He loves big men.

His tantrums now are connected mostly with his social inter-actions. He is not willing to display (or capable of displaying?) such traits of character as tolerance, patience, turn-taking or com-promise.

He learns the word "win" and wants to be a winner at anything he does. Usually he wants to be the only winner.

He loves pushing children and watching them fall. He thinks this is quite funny; yet he does it without malice. He is not a bully: he will push big children, little children, whoever is available. He enjoys interaction with other children, but he just doesn't know any other way to achieve it. He doesn't realize that he might hurt someone.

He knows the alphabet. He has started reading three-letter words – cat, fat, bat, mat, and so on. He still likes being read to, as long as the reading is theatrical and animated. But left to his own devices, he'd rather watch television, and plenty of it.

We're pressed to enforce intense potty training because his school is not set up to deal with accidents. We succeed. Finally he can take care of his own toileting.

Because Billy pushes (and bites and scratches too), we still take our children to playgrounds that are mostly empty. Billy interacts well enough with Francesca, who knows his ways and is tolerant. Usually they have a good time when there is no one else around. But if there is a newcomer, for Billy the playground becomes a tournament ground where he is compelled to prove his knighthood. As a rule I get the children into the car and leave before he gets a chance to do it.

His impersonations of dragons and other scary creatures continue and are a persistent irritant to everyone around him.

I learn to deal with some of his temper tantrums. I become aware that, for the first time, in some ways I can affect Billy.

At the end of his sixth year

Billy finishes first grade. He has shown such limited academic and mental abilities that I question how much he will ever learn. Frustrated, I decide to test his capacities for myself. I organize a daily summer school of our own, three hours each morning for two months. It's a stressful endeavor but a worthwhile one, for it becomes clear to me that he can learn readily on a one-on-one basis. Much of his apparent inability to learn results from his limited attention-span. It is frustrating to try to get him to focus, but I discover that, once I have his attention, he can understand concepts and can remember what he's been taught. Math is a struggle for both of us, but he learns to read easily and develops a taste for it. I describe this summer school at length in Chapter 41.

At seven

Billy goes to second grade, again to a special-education classroom. His social interaction improved during the summer, but now, as he is surrounded exclusively by other children with behavioral problems, it gets worse again. (A typical day in his special-education class is described in Chapters 40 and 42, where I discuss special-education schooling in more detail.)

Despairing of special education, I take Billy out of the school system. I am going to teach him at home.

Billy responds very well to our home school, both behaviorally and intellectually. We reduce the amount of noises that he is making. In about eight weeks we reduce his impersonations of dragons to a bearable minimum. He quickly learns how to read at first-grade level, and by the end of the year he is reading at second-grade level.

He also begins to make progress in math. By the end of the year Billy does problems that involve carrying numbers, in both addition and subtraction, although he still has a hard time with conceptual problems such as time and money.

His social skills improve. He no longer shows aggressive behaviors such as biting and scratching. He still likes to push, but he is willing to admit that it's not a nice thing to do.

His temper tantrums are much milder as he and I jointly become more and more artful at redirecting them. Instead of building to a raging torrent, they flow out into calmer and calmer pools.

I start to take him to church on Sundays. He learns about God.

His church behavior is bearable, as long as someone sits with him. Otherwise, he is prone to misbehave. He finds it boring to sit and do nothing, and he entertains himself by making faces at people around him, sliding out of his seat or climbing on it, and jumping up and down during hymn-singing. But the good Christians of our church gladly tolerate him.

By the end of the year Billy volunteers to say a prayer at dinner. An example: "Dear God, thank you for this lovely food, thank you for being kind and creating our bodies, thank you for the Earf, and Jesus we love you very much. O Man." This is a short prayer, for Billy. Sometimes he goes on for several minutes. We are astonished to discover that he is a natural preacher.

He learns to enjoy new foods like corn, cauliflower, and broccoli. More additions to his menu: peaches, grapes, popcorn, corn chips (blue corn with sesame seeds – organic!). He is very fond of chicken legs, which I bake with spices. He branches out as far as eating fresh bread with melted butter.

We made wonderful progress during this year.

At eight

Billy is becoming a different person. When we celebrate his birthday on August 31, we celebrate much more than eight years of living on Earth. We celebrate a beautiful soul which finally is opening to other people. We celebrate the joy which Billy has brought into our lives. We celebrate the greatness of God, for it seems he has arranged for Billy a journey which was meant to touch many hearts.

After Labor Day we resume our home schooling program.

At the beginning of October Billy undergoes three comprehensive tests given by the school district, tests designed to measure the academic proficiency of normal students. Billy's performance in all subjects is at least average for his age, and in several he performs well above his age. His reading is at an age level of about nine-and-a-half years. Hooray!

Now, at eight-and-a-half, as this book is being written, Billy reads at third-grade level. He loves prefixes and suffixes. We're studying maps and talking about traveling the world. He can add and subtract four-digit numbers and he's learning the multiplication table. And he's very fond of fractions. Isn't everybody?

13

A Guardian Angel

It is obvious from the previous chapter that Billy's major social and academic gains happened only recently, during the time I've home-schooled him. Schooling Billy at home has given me an opportunity to teach him one-on-one, to experiment with different learning approaches, to have a personal curriculum for him and to adjust that curriculum daily based on his performance.

I started as a poor teacher with little tolerance for either interruptions or misbehavior. But my desire to succeed was so strong that I worked hard to make myself a better teacher. I worked hard to uncover every little bit of information that somehow could help Billy and me.

I learned from books about autism, psychology, and mental control. I learned from focused self-observation. I learned from school psychologists, speech therapists, occupational therapists and classroom teachers.

But my main learning began with and was supported by Theresa. She was Billy's preschool teacher and his first real teacher. Before her, I don't think either my husband or I really taught Billy, and I know his day-care teachers didn't. We only herded him. We kept him out of the worst forests and thickets he might have found himself in; but we didn't teach him to find his own way out. Theresa was the one to make a major breakthrough in his development. At a time when he couldn't yet talk, she was confident he would talk, and started him talking. Where others saw Billy as a wild thing, she saw an intelligent, imaginative, and dramatic boy. And she was the one who discovered that he understood logic. She said, a few months after he started her preschool class, "I think he'll go to college."

Theresa made step-by-step instruction books just for Billy. None of the other children in her classroom at the time responded to that method. Yet Billy loved to follow page by page, to look at the pictured instructions and follow them by doing what was shown. For example, planting a seed: the first page had a drawing of dirt being poured into the pot; the next showed a seed being planted; next it is covered with more dirt; next it is watered. This was a simple book. Theresa designed many others for Billy, more complicated.

Billy long ago graduated from Theresa's class. He's been to other schools with other teachers. Yet I keep going back to her classroom, a room filled with toys, with games, with a vast variety of devices to strike a spark in a four-year-old special-ed mind. It is magical to watch Theresa use her endless creativity in devising ways to start each child learning. She is a guardian angel not just to Billy, but to every child who is fortunate enough to come into her classroom.

I've seen Theresa create personalized seating arrangements for children who spend much of their time making repetitive motions. A boy who was continually hurting his head ended up sitting on a throne of firm foam cushions. They protected him from hurting himself, yet allowed him to have a little raised desk in front of him so he could color and do other tasks.

To distract children who chewed on their clothes or other items, she provided creative work. Many autistic children have extremely heightened sensory perceptions. The world may literally be painful to them. For them, her classroom was a refuge of calming variety. My favorite feature of her classroom was a deep table where the children could play with multicolored rice. The bright colors made the rice attractive, and yet the feel of it was very soothing.

One of my favorite times to observe Theresa's classroom was circle time. She had a remarkable ability to control the attention of a group of children whose individual attentions flew like wild birds. Every portion of her circle time was a performance, and every performance was carefully dramatized. Shapes, colors and music were an integral part of her presentations, as was an element of surprise. She was uniquely good at this; but her techniques can be used successfully by other people. I try to follow her example in teaching Billy.

This Dragon is black Because horse.N.

14

My First Step in Managing Billy – "Buying Time"

It was from Theresa that I learned my first technique in dealing with Billy's tantrums.

Her classroom was divided into sections – play area, circle area, area for table activities. These areas were separated by shelves, and some of the entrances to them were quite narrow. Theresa showed me how, when Billy didn't want to finish a task and tried to escape from the area, she just would not let him out. She would put a little chair in the entrance, sit on it and do what I came to call "buying time." Billy could not stand the idea that he had to do anything he didn't want to do. But there was no way out. Theresa, whom he liked very much, sat in the entrance, composed and friendly, just repeating words of encouragement: "You just have to finish your task, Billy. I know it's hard, I understand how you feel, but I don't think I can move from here unless you finish. I just can't move. I want to get up and do something else, and I'd be glad to do it as soon as you're done. But not before."

I was amazed at the simplicity of "buying time" and amazed that it worked. For it to work, of course, the adult must have the patience to sit there and block the way out until the child complies. And the adult must be able to maintain a steady friendliness in her voice all the while her autistic child is going through the different stages of his protest.

My own first "buying time" sessions were about not letting Billy watch television in the living room and making him go to bed at a certain time.

We had struggled practically every evening about going upstairs to bed. Often my husband and I would just give up the fight and settle for a quiet evening and a child who falls asleep while watching television and is carried peacefully upstairs.

One evening, after another unsuccessful attempt to urge Billy to let go of the television, I grabbed him, carried him upstairs to his room, went in with him, closed the door and sat blocking the door with my back. I took a deep breath, closed my eyes for a moment trying to become aware of my own voice, and started buying time.

I had to buy about forty minutes; and every one of them was painful for both of us. As Billy was going through different stages of rage, crying, throwing himself on the floor, trying to push me away from the door, I tried hard to stay calm and kept repeating that I loved him very much, that he is my sweet boy, that he has to go to bed in his room at 8:30, that there was nothing that I could do to change it, and that I was going to sit there as long as it took him to go nicely to bed in his room. Eventually, he gave up his theatrics. He got into bed and went to sleep.

The magic of "buying time" is simple – after a while the child gets tired. A tantrum takes a lot of energy, both physical and emotional. It is my observation with Billy that at the time when he had regular strong tantrums he could sustain one for about thirty minutes. The tantrum would reach a peak, and after that it would slowly subside. It was obvious how tired he was, from his voice, his eyes, and all the muscles of his little body. After thirty minutes he was ready to be held and comforted.

Before I learned to "buy time," I tended to try to comfort Billy very early in the tantrum. The tantrum was hard on me, too, so I attempted to stop it by offering compromises, only to succumb to almost everything he insisted on. "Buying time" was not "being hard on the boy." "Buying time" was a strategy that made sense and had a very specific target: to end a tantrum. It was definitely worth the effort.

One important thing that I learned from "buying time" is that Billy really didn't like his tantrums. He used them to protest a situation that displeased him. He used tantrums to get what he wanted – but only as long as they worked. When he realized that in certain circumstances his tantrums didn't get the desired result, he stopped throwing tantrums in those circumstances.

In the case of evening television viewing, it took us about two weeks to have Billy go to his room without protesting. The first "buying time," as I've described, was quite agonizing for both of us. But those that followed took less and less time and were less and less intense.

Progress made my heart rejoice.

From then on, every time I needed to shut off a tantrum, I'd pull myself together, make myself firm, and chant my love and encouragement. Through all the tears and the protests I'd repeat gently that he has to accept the rules, because that's the way life is. And eventually he accepted. That's the way life is.

It is important to say that parents should be sure that they understand the reason for a tantrum before they try to combat it. Earlier I wrote that little Billy used to throw tantrums every time I'd try to put him into his car seat. I had many guesses about the reasons for these tantrums. "Maybe he hates the ride." "Maybe he hates leaving the house." But in fact, he just couldn't stand having his pants legs pulled above his socks. Once I realized this, I easily averted the tantrum just by making sure that his pants always covered his socks.

Once you've identified the cause of a tantrum, it's important to plan in advance the words you'll use to "buy time," because it's hard to be wisely creative in the excitement of a tantrum. Your speech to your child should include three subjects:

- why not to do a certain thing
- what is to be done instead
- "support language."

Why not to do a certain thing

You should give a reason; and it should be a reason that will make sense (and be convincing) to a child. I don't tell Billy that he's not allowed to watch television "because Mom says so;" I tell him that I've talked to his doctor and asked how much time a child of his age should spend watching television, and I have to abide by the doctor's recommendation because I want a healthy boy. "Wouldn't you do the same for your child?" I ask Billy.

What is to be done instead

Offer options that are appealing to the child. When I first started training Billy not to watch television, I had no option to offer him other than to read a book. The transition became easier when I started to offer him a tray with a night-time snack along with his book.

Support language

When we started "buying time" to calm Billy's tantrums, his vocabulary was still limited. At best it was at the level of a typical three-year-old (Billy was five). It was important to use only words and expression that made complete sense to him. My task was to find words that Billy knew and understood in a very specific way.

In choosing "support language" for a disturbed child, eloquence is beside the point. If the only support word that the child knows is "love," then your speech should include the word "love" over and over. To bring some variety into the speech (to avoid boring yourself, more than boring the child), vary the intonation, the amplitude, the pitch. You might sing this word, proclaim it, or whisper it intimately. Remember, it can take a long time, especially at the beginning, to get past the peak of a tantrum. It will help you greatly if you prepare in your own mind how you'll handle the whole journey, both verbally and emotionally.

15

Rituals

And so, after long effort, we succeeded at the "simple" task of sending Billy to bed in his room at a certain time. Later we succeeded in actually getting Billy to enjoy going to his room to bed.

A large part of this success came from developing a bedtime ritual. This was one of the first rituals that I designed. Since then we have developed many others. Some of them served only for a short time and withered away. Others have become an integral part of our lives. Some have become a great source of security for Billy. The anticipation of something very familiar tends to make anyone comfortable and relaxed. And how often can we say about an autistic child that something makes him comfortable and relaxed?

In my home country, in the old days travelers stopped for a rest whenever they reached a well. The well was the signal that it was time to sit down and relax, to eat and drink and be grateful. With Billy, our rituals became these wells of relaxation.

Rituals, of course, have been a part of our Earth since antiquity.

I was brought up in Moldavia, a republic in the southern part of the USSR, in the '60s and '70s. It was a time of great change for my homeland. Rituals that had shaped people's lives for years started to die out quickly, giving way to new customs brought in by the Communists.

The women stopped baking bread at home and started to buy bread from stores. The traditional three-day-long weddings, which had marked a couple's transition into a new stage of life, became a Saturday-night bash at the town cafeteria. Craftwork became just a waste of time. Herb-lore and the collection of wild herbs gave way to whatever turned up at the pharmacy.

I loved the old rituals, and still do. Maybe I love them because they once brought me a sense of belonging. I loved when my nanny would take me to the houses in town where several women were working on a rug. The women sang as they worked, and their hands moved the yarn so fast, it was as if the hands were singing a song as well. And I loved when women of the neighborhood got together for a chat on a Sunday night. They ate sunflower seeds and rocked their children. And there was so much peace, so much love.

Years later, when I moved to the United States, I discovered to my astonishment that, no matter how many rituals had died in Russia, the Russian people still have kept many more of them than most Americans have. The only rituals many Americans grow up with are Thanksgiving turkey and Christmas presents.

A ritual, as I see it, has a spiritual component. It is designed to dignify certain parts of our lives, to enhance their importance. Rituals are designed to pass something on to another generation. They are structures around which we build our memories and our progress in life. Rituals, when they involve several or more people, become a magical unifying force.

Our bedtime ritual was simple, but Billy loved it so much that three years later we are still following it. First, he takes a bath. Second, he puts on his pajamas. And third, he gets a tray of food to carry with him to his room and into his bed.

Every part should be done with perfection, and every part has its own details of recognition. It is the details of recognition that make a ritual powerful.

These are the details of our bedtime ritual.

1. We put a stool by the bath tub. The stool is inviting and makes it possible for Billy to step into the tub with dignity. We make sure that every night a large, soft, dry towel is spread from the floor onto the stool – an improvised walkway to an improvised throne. He finds it appealing to progress over the towel instead of walking on the cold tiles of the bathroom floor.

    Around the tub is a variety of toys which he can reach while he is in the water. It is important to make sure that once in a while he finds a "surprise" toy waiting for him among the others. That makes the bath ever so desirable. And there are the sponges. They can be used as a part of the ritual as well. How? Get two or three sponges, all different. Then use the green one (for example) to wash his face, the blue one his body, and the red one his feet. You can also invent a different song for each sponge. Soon the child is eager to participate and hands you the right sponge for the right part of the body.

    The towel for drying is waiting on the floor. It is large and soft.

2. Done with the bath, we move into Billy's room. His pajamas are already spread on the rug together with clean underwear. Once he is in his pajamas, he is told to choose three books from the bookshelf in his room. Billy has more than a hundred books at a time in his room. We move them around a lot, and he likes to redis-cover long-forgotten books. Then he takes the books to

bed, and I go to the kitchen to fetch his night-time snack.

3. We use a plastic tray for his snack. I joke that he gets served like a Turkish pasha. He likes the joke every time.

   His tray consistently must have three things: "cut apples, cut carrots, and full cup of apple juice," Billy says. It is a ritual incantation.

   As an adult reads the three books to him (or, more recently, with him), Billy munches on his snack. When we're done, we leave the night light on and turn on some soothing music. Billy gets his night-time kiss and, with a sense of completion, cuddles into his soft blanket. He buries his nose in his teddy's soft coat and is off to sweet dreams.

4. This part is for the nights when Billy does not want to be left alone. Most often he is ready for sleep; but if not, I sit on the bed next to him and gently massage his forehead between his eyebrows.

   I once told Billy that long ago there was a Turkish pasha who won many battles. After every battle, he'd come home tired to Istanbul, to his beautiful princess. He'd lie down, put his head in her arms, and close his eyes. And she'd touch him, gently – "just like this," I said, demonstrating. Ever since, when I refer to "the Princess Touch," Billy remembers the story, and he knows what comes next – a gentle touch between his eyebrows that puts him to sleep.

   "The Princess Touch" is powerful. It makes one very, very sleepy. Billy too.

I can envision being questioned about the wisdom of letting a child eat and drink in bed right before going to sleep. While I am not an advocate of eating before bedtime, I've found it very acceptable in Billy's case. First of all, when his diet was stuck on pizza, hot dogs and macaroni and cheese, the bedtime snack became an important source of vitamins. Second, the process of eating is itself a calming and comforting process. There's a good reason that babies fall asleep while sucking milk.

For us, the night-time snack was a reasonable tradeoff. It helped Billy make the transition from the day to the night. With apples and carrots as snacks, I could see no reason to deny him and us the comfort of an uneventful, predictable bedtime. I don't think this ritual will last for too many years. At some point, especially when Billy becomes involved in reading adventure books, I can see him skipping his "night-time snack in the bed" now and then, and at last giving it up for good.

As I said, this ritual has been with us for a long time. It goes the same way whether Billy is put to bed by me, by my husband or by our occasional sitter.

The same goes for bath time. Billy will easily comply with an adult as long as the person in charge is familiar and follows the ritual. Just recently our daughter, who is ten years old, started helping us with parts of the ritual.

One particular ritual became very special for us.

I mentioned before that Billy started to talk only when he was four. His vocabulary increased quite slowly between the ages of four and six. After age six, his rate of acquiring new words increased substantially.

At six Billy had a basic household vocabulary. He knew words that catered to his immediate needs. But besides these words, at the age of six he was already trained to understand and use the following concepts:

- to be proud
- to promise
- to give his word
- to keep a promise
- to keep his word
- word of honor
- solemnly.

I taught him these notions first of all by keeping my own promises and by stressing the whole process of making a promise and then the process of keeping it. I made him pay attention when I was giving my word and made him realize that I was bound by it.

I made sure that promising and the giving of a word were not overused, but rather were reserved for special occasions. I designed a little ritual for making a promise. It goes like this:

1. We discuss the issue, and I ask Billy if he can promise a certain thing. If Billy is ready to go ahead with the promise, we proceed to step 2.

2. Billy and I raise our right hands.

3. I ask him to repeat after me the words of the promise. They are fit for a proud medieval knight. For example: "I hereby solemnly promise to choose only one movie at Blockbuster. I will keep my promise with honor."

4. We put our hands on our hearts.

5. Billy, hand on his heart, says, "I solemnly promise."

5. We both bow.

6. We put our hands down. The promise is completed.

Sometimes we've had to go through the promise ritual in the car. I make sure to sustain the dramatic aura of the ritual. Once in a while I've had to make cross faces at the same time, as when Francesca giggled because Billy couldn't say "solemnly." I just went on, encouraging him gently: "It's OK, Billy. SO-LEM-LY. SO-LEM-LY." He knows how to say this word very well now.

Our boy keeps his word better than many grown men and women I know. He feels empowered by the responsibility that he takes on at his own will, the responsibility for keeping his word. And it's beautiful to watch how happy he is to have this power.

Our rituals are a good method of keeping track of Billy's progress. When you keep up a consistent procedure for a year or two, you're bound to notice when he is ready to accept some change in the routine.

Things to remember when designing a ritual:

1. *It should consist of only a few simple steps.*

2. *The sequence from one step to another should be clearly defined.*

3. *The steps should be designed in such a way that different people will have no problems in following the ritual.* For example, I would not advise arranging a night-time ritual around a song that is sung live by someone with a voice so beautiful that it becomes a hard act to follow. Better to have that song taped and to organize the ritual around the tape. That will make it easier for adults to take turns in following the ritual.

emperer
Devil Dragon

Here are some other rituals we have used:

Morning ritual. For getting Billy ready in the morning I designed a board that lists his major tasks in getting ready for the day. The board has Velcro-backed cards that are torn off (and deposited in a pocket at the bottom of the board) to show when Billy has completed each task. More will be said about this board in Chapter 16.

But note that there's a difference between a ritual and a schedule. For me, a ritual is a dramatized implementation of a certain segment of a schedule. We lay out Billy's clean clothes on the rug in his room, arranged in the order in which he puts them on. When I wake the children, I turn on some rhythmic music. I usually prefer New Age or tunes inspired by folk music; but once in a while I go for something powerful, such as Orff's *Carmina Burana.* It gets them out of bed and moving.

Taking a bath has sometimes been a part of our morning ritual as well. That amounts to two baths a day, but it pays off if it makes the boy's life easier.

For several years, getting up was a stressful time for Billy. He would hide under his blanket, not willing to get out. He'd pretend to be a hiding puppy, a cozy kitten and many other creatures of his abundant imagination. At the same time, the clock was running; and by the time I finally could get him out of bed, my stress level was already high.

Then I figured out that the reason he was hiding under the blanket was that the bed was warm and cozy, while the room outside the blanket was not so warm and cozy. (I ought to tell you that when I "discover" simple things like this, I feel quite stupid. Billy's adaptation to the world has not needed the help of rocket science. It has been helped by formulas of the most down-to-earth simplicity – formulas which come not so much from the analytical part of the brain as from pure compassion.)

Once I understood Billy's trouble with reality (the room is colder than the bed), I started to wake him up by telling him that there is a bath full of warm, wonderful water waiting for him. It made a big difference. Billy didn't hide under his blankets any more.

A bath in the morning put an additional strain on time management. But I just moved the waking time about fifteen minutes earlier. I also made clear to my children that while the evening bath didn't have a set time limit, the morning one did. I use music to help set time limits. I give the children a couple of songs or a passage of familiar music as a guideline for getting out of the tub. It works wonderfully well. It works because, once the limit is set, they have to get out of the tub not because I say so, but because they've used up their allotted time.

Breakfast. Our day's first meal is ritualized as well. It's important to offer Billy a choice, but he gets a limited number of choices. (See Chapter 18 on the use of choices.) Billy's choices for breakfast are:

- toasted peanut-butter-and-jelly sandwich
- cereal with milk (he will accept multigrain Cheerios only)
- chocolate muffin.

We ordinarily do not allow any variations. Otherwise the morning may turn into a long process of negotiation.

Scheduling a week

In general our day is highly structured. Time is allocated for school, homework, meals, play, television, and reading. In addition, practically every day has its own definite schedule for the leftover time.

Monday nights we go to story time at our local book store.

Tuesday we have an early dinner, before our daughter goes to gymnastics. Most of the time Billy joins a parent in getting Francesca to and from the gym. We also spend some time watching the gymnasts practice.

Wednesday is an open night.

Thursday is a short day at school. The four of us meet together for lunch at a local university's cafeteria. The food is good and the dining area overlooks the ocean. Again, it's a gymnastics night.

Friday mom and dad go out. Our long-time babysitter comes to join the children for a night of pizza, a rented movie, and popcorn.

Saturday mornings we go to the "Russian park," where Francesca studies Russian for two hours with a small group of children of Russian descent. Billy has always refused to learn Russian (Francesca was bilingual from the time she began to talk), but he loves to go along and play in the park. While Francesca studies, I help Billy improve his social skills by making verbal and emotional links between him and whatever other children happen to be playing in the park. We've been visiting our "Russian park" every Saturday for four years now, and we have made a lot of progress. Billy has grown able to maintain friendly relationships with the boys from the neighborhood. Where in the beginning I had to monitor all of Billy's steps and actions, now I can sit on a bench with a magazine and keep an eye from afar just to make sure that there are no ego clashes.

Saturday is also most often an out-for-lunch day, followed by playtime. Saturday evening we have family entertainment – a video, friends for dinner, or reading by a fire in cold weather.

Sunday morning we dress up and go to church. At the church, Billy's ritual is to promise to walk and not run, to hold his sister's hand, and to be quiet. The two of them walk to the area of the church where all of the children sit together. Billy is usually restless until some other boys come: he refuses to sit with girls and acts as if it's beneath his dignity to do so. With enough boys around and the choir singing, Billy gets caught up in the rhythm of the service.

After church, Billy is allowed to say a prayer at lunch – as long a prayer as he wants (which can sometimes be quite long). His prayers are what we call *vitievato* in Russian, which my dictionary translates as "ornate, flowery, florid, rhetorical." I'm sure God loves them as much as we do.

It is important for Billy that Sunday be a day of rest. I try to avoid excitement and to remind him often that tomorrow is Monday: school again. It's better to start preparing him long in advance for this major transition. Sometimes I overdo the preparation, to the point that Billy says, "I know! I know, Mom! I know it's going to be Monday!"

Such continuing day-to-day, week-to-week structure, combined with rituals, helps to reduce the stress of raising an autistic child, both for the child and the parents.

16

Schedules

It is common for autistic children to be slaves to their routines. They do the same things at the same times. Variations and innovations are not welcome.

At first, this dedication to a routine may seem yet another yoke for the parents of an autistic child. But if we learn to use it to help the child (for example, to learn new words and new behaviors), this dedication can be a blessing.

The hard part is adopting a new routine. It may take several weeks before a child will first accept a change and then become dedicated to it.

Mornings

I've already described how hard our mornings used to be. When Billy awoke, he didn't want to recognize that he had to get ready for the day. He'd try to hide under his blanket, then refuse to brush his teeth, then try to avoid getting dressed. The routine of a warm bath every morning solved the problem of fishing him from under his blanket; but everything else was still a problem.

I didn't solve this problem of morning obstruction until Billy was six. Then I realized I could take charge. I made a colorful pictorial schedule for the morning and hung it on the wall outside Billy's door.

Billy's morning schedule has drawings of Billy doing each of his chores: brushing his teeth, washing his face, washing his ears, putting on his clothes, having his breakfast.

The picture of every chore has next to it a square containing a card saying "NOT DONE YET." The card is attached with Velcro. When Billy is finished with a chore, he can remove that card and put it into a little pouch at the bottom of the poster. Underneath that card, the square now visible says "OH YES I'M DONE."

Billy used this schedule faithfully every day for about a year, and then he outgrew it. At age eight, he hasn't used his morning schedule in a year. He still does all his tasks, in order; but the schedule is now in his mind. But for a year or more, the picture board was his guide to getting ready for the day.

The important thing about this type of schedule is that the child interacts with it. It is not just a list of orders on the wall. Billy loved running to it, pulling off the "NOT DONE YET" cards and throwing them into the pouch. He loved declaring victoriously, "OH YES I'M DONE."

Once a routine is established, the next problem is likely to be...changing it. Life changes; autistic kids don't. Or they resent doing it. But Billy's morning schedule was also a big help in adding new tasks to his morning routine. After several months of using the basic morning schedule, I drew a new one. This one contained all the old tasks plus a new card for making the bed, another one for combing his hair, and, most important of all, a third with the instruction "SMILE!"

I hung the schedule and went to bed wondering what Billy's reaction would be in the morning. Morning was wonderful. Billy went to his schedule, and he paused as his eyes took in the newness of it. Then he said gleefully, "Mom, I need to make my bed now! Can you help me? And I need a comb to comb my hair!" Then he turned his face to me, smiling to his ears, and said, "See my smile?" Then he turned back to the schedule, pulled off the card that said "NOT DONE YET" by the smiley face, and said, "Oh, yes, I'm done!"

It was that simple. Oh, the blessing of an autistic child's dedication to his schedule.

Billy's morning schedule made Francesca envious. She wanted one too, and made one for herself. But she never really used it. She went through the motions a few times; but the schedule had no hold on her. Typical children do not depend on routines as much as autistic children. The "make your bed" card on Francesca's schedule had far less influence on her than Billy's did on him, because she has no feeling that a schedule is binding on her. Francesca (like most typical children) has no difficulty in just skipping over a step, or skipping the whole thing. I think that, instead of being unsettled, she has a sneaky feeling of triumph: she's got away with something. Billy has no easy access to such an emotion. He has to be prepared in advance for any change.

Playgrounds

I've told you how hard it was for Billy to fit in with other children at a playground. It was hard enough that, soon after we moved to San Diego, I decided to avoid the problem by avoiding other children. I analyzed the number of visitors, and their usual visiting times, at all the playgrounds within a half-hour's drive from our house. Then I arranged to visit playgrounds only when there was unlikely to be anyone else there – just Billy, Francesca, and me. Then I could drink my coffee.

Eventually, as Billy matured and acquired language, I started training him to play with other children. When he was six, I began taking him to playgrounds while other children were there; but I dedicated my time to spotting boys who might be willing to play with him. Then I'd introduce myself and talk to them about Billy. I'd tell my new little friends that Billy could play only a few games and that he didn't know many words, but if they were willing to play dragons, they'd have a great time.

Once in a while I was lucky enough to find a boy who'd say, "Dragons? I'll play dragons!" Billy was good at playing dragons. Soon every participant would have a dragon name and a dragon color. And they'd pretend to fly, spreading their arms as wings. There'd be a pretend castle to be protected, as well as the eggs with new baby dragons in them to protect from pretend enemies. Fire was blown from their mouths, and smoke covered the sky.

Then came pirate games, and I trained boys about how Billy played pirates.

Little by little we ventured onto populated playgrounds. Sometimes I could even drink coffee, even if there were other children on the playground; but I still kept two eyes on the course of the games, ready to arbitrate a quarrel between pirates as to who's to be captain of the ship.

An even better solution came when I designed a "playground behavior" schedule for Billy. This was a folding card with drawings on both sides. On one side were instructions about social interaction: "BE NICE," "SHARE," and so on. On the other side I had three happy faces as well as three free-standing cards with sad faces. Every time we went to the playground, Billy and I reviewed the folding card before I'd let him get out of the car. First we repeated the rules. Then I reminded him that every time he broke a rule, a sad face would be placed on top of the happy face. If all three happy faces got covered, Billy would get in the car, and we would drive home.

At the playground I followed Billy with the folding card in my hands, and every time I placed a sad face, I made sure he understood what it was for. I also made sure he knew how many happy faces were left.

The success with this card was outstanding. Before I began using it, if Billy's behavior became impossible to bear and I had to inform him that we were going home, he would be outraged. Often I'd have to drag him to the car.

The card organized his attitude. He did not like to see a happy face covered: it was a visible reminder that his playtime was in danger. Sometimes three faces were covered, and we had to leave. Sometimes he cried if that happened; but he gave me much less trouble than he would have before the card came into our lives. And generally he was able to hang on through a whole playground session without getting three sad faces.

I was letting him participate in creating his future.

It can be painful to acknowledge that we create our future with our own hands. This acknowledgment has brought, at one time or another, existential pain to every adult I know.

The playground card was Billy's first acquaintance with this profound responsibility for his own future. It was no longer I who was responsible for his having to leave the playground. As painful as it was for him to admit, he had his future in his own hands. And he knew it.

Changes in schedules

As I've noted, each of our days has a simple and settled routine. But when we must have some deviation from the routine, and I anticipate that Billy might resist, I write the new schedule with colorful markers on a board on our kitchen wall. If Billy sees a schedule in writing, with times for the beginning and end of each activity, the probability that he will accept it is greatly increased.

Again, it's a chore for the parent to think about the schedule in advance, to organize it in words, to write the words neatly on the board.

Look at it as a craft – a part of the craft of raising an autistic child.

17

Communicating in Poetry

As we now know, autistic children do not like deviations from their routine. If the child is expecting apples as a night-time snack, you'd better have the apples ready. Otherwise...

I used to deal with Billy's "otherwise..." in all sorts of clumsy ways. Since then, I've learned to create poetic communication.

I remember the night when I went to the kitchen to prepare Billy's night-time snack and found there were no apples in the refrigerator. I went upstairs and told Billy that I had four things to tell him.

Number one – an accident happened and all the apples disappeared from the refrigerator.

Number two – I am very sorry and I ask him to forgive me for letting it happen.

Number three – I ask him to accept a tradeoff, some fresh and tasty grapes with no seeds.

Number four – I promise to buy delicious apples the very next day.

I watched, with delight, how the expressions of Billy's little face changed as I went through the four points. His face changed from grumpy and disappointed to negotiating to acceptance. I asked him if we could make a deal and, if we could, would that be a thumb deal or a pinkie deal. We settled for a thumb deal. Then I took a piece of paper and told him that this was my shopping list. I wrote "APPLES" on it in big letters.

I kept my promise. The next day I bought the apples. But from then on I was always aware that if there is any deviation from a routine, I need to have a plan that is thought out very carefully before I approach Billy with disappointing news. The verbal part needs to be created like a poem. And it had better be created in advance, for, when dealing with an autistic child, each word is important and spontaneity is no substitute for calmness.

The poem needs to have a beginning, a turning-point and an emotional completion. It is a little drama. And if you play your part right, it works.

Here are some important criteria for the poem, or the verbal plan:

> *First, state how many things the child will be told.* Autistic children don't like to listen. But if they must listen, it is much easier for them to organize their attention when they have advance notice of what they will be listening to, so that they themselves can keep track of the progress. It gives them a sense of control, which makes them feel good, which helps them listen.
>
> As my husband tells me, the Army's procedure for giving instruction to the troops was: "Tell them what you're going to tell them; tell them; and tell them what you told them."
>
> It also helps to place in front of the child (and the troops too, no doubt) several small objects, interesting enough to catch their attention (but not interesting enough to completely distract them), corresponding to the number of points you're going to cover.
>
> For example, if the child is to be told four things, then place four marbles (blocks, cotton balls, etc.) next to him.

Every time you're finished with telling one thing, he gets to remove one item.

Second, state the problem. This should be brief. When I state the problem, I like to get my voice into a declamatory mode and give it as much pathos as possible – something like telling a king that the enemy's envoy is there to see him. When the child hears such a voice, he elevates his attention and is a little disturbed by it. So it comes as a great relief when you suddenly change the voice to a soft tone coming from the heart and…

Third, offer a graceful apology. I like to apologize in a dramatic way. Billy is very familiar with apologies, since from the beginning of his time he's done so many things wrong and has been asked to apologize far more frequently than typical children. So it pleases him to hear a dramatic, oversized apology addressed to him. At the same time he knows, somehow, that I'm not entirely serious about the whole thing. So as I go on apologizing, he begins to smile. This is a very important moment. The moment he smiles, I know he's not going to have a temper tantrum. The disturbing news, whatever it may be, will not be a cause for tragedy.

From here on the rest of the poetry goes smoothly and requires much less dramatic effort from my part.

Fourth, state the tradeoff. The tradeoff should be fair.

Fifth, make a promise that states exactly what will be done to solve the problem and exactly when.

18

ChOT (The "Choice-Offering Tool")

One of the first things one learns when managing an autistic child is the importance of "choice." I started offering choices to Billy when he was in preschool. I was amazed at the power of "choice" as a tool. I was grateful. After all, "choice" saved me from slavery. For I did feel like a slave at times when I approached my sweet boy, asking him to join us for dinner, to get out of bed or to take a bath, and encountered an unapproachable, unresponsive, uncommuni-cative and uncooperative attitude. So no wonder I have a sense of magic in using ChOT (the "Choice-Offering Tool").

I use the term "ChOT" instead of just "choice" because the term "choice" causes most people (me too) to think it's either this or that – two choices, with little thought. This often won't do if you're trying to train an autistic child. "ChOT" requires the offering of choices designed in advance to accomplish a certain task, whether it's to change a behavior or to learn a new word. *ChOT is designed for training.* The choices in ChOT are not necessarily the ones that first come to mind. Advance planning is required to decide how many choices to offer and which ones. For example, if you're offering a choice of socks, you need to think about what colors you will offer, what designs (the ones with cars? the ones with dragons?), and how many pairs you'll lay out.

The principle of ChOT is simple. But coming up with choices fifty times a day is not simple. Not every parent manages to take

ChOT to that extent. But, taken to that extent, it becomes a powerful tool.

I started implementing ChOT when Billy was four. His diet was poor. He rejected all culinary offerings beyond a list of eight things, and those eight included apple juice and soda. We were ready to rejoice at the acceptance of pretty much any new food, whether it was organic or not. So when I put two hot dogs in front of Billy and asked him if he would prefer to eat one hot dog or two hot dogs, and he said, "One hot dog," my heart leaped with joy.

It was a long time before he accepted another new food, but that first success with ChOT encouraged me to use it in all sorts of ways.

The next success with ChOT was with dressing in the morning. It used to be a horrible time for Billy and me. Using ChOT, I started preparing two sets of clothes for him. When he got up, I would ask him pleasantly:

"Would you like the socks with baseballs or the socks with lions?"

"Which pants would you like to put on, the soft ones or the jeans?"

"Would you like to put on the sweatshirt or the button-down shirt?"

At the time when I started using ChOT, Billy barely spoke. So he just pointed to the socks with lions on them, to the soft pants or to the sweatshirt. Whether he pointed or spoke, it was amazing to have him actually make a choice – have him accept the choices that were offered – instead of fighting against everything.

The most important trick about ChOT is to make sure that one choice is significantly more appealing than any of the others. Billy likes lions much better than baseballs, and soft clothes better than scratchy ones. Your child's taste may be different; but, whatever it is, try to make one choice a favorite. That will help your child decide quickly.

Autistic children seem to come into this world rejecting all the rules of communication that humanity has laboriously built up over thousands of years. Not only do they hate what they don't want to do; they have no fear and care nothing about what others think.

At the same time, *they do not like to have tantrums.* And this is a very important point. *They really do not like to have tantrums.* They would rather avoid them, if only they knew how. Tantrums are a rejection of reality at moments when they don't know how else to react.

Autistic children have a magnificent inner world. So magnificent is it that they would rather spend all their time in that magnificent inner world than have to deal with the ways of human civilization. Often, things that amuse the rest of us are not amusing to them; chores that seem necessary to the rest of us do not seem necessary to them; what entertains the rest of us means nothing to them.

And so the process of living, for an autistic child (God bless his/her soul!), comes down to being endlessly forced to participate in things which do not make sense and are often plain unpleasant.

If you have an autistic child, you have a child who is not looking to his mother for suggestions about what to do. You have a child who never stops insisting on his own agenda.

Autistic children did not come into this world to please adults. We have non-autistic children to do that, the children who do not oppose or even question their parents. The children who seek praise, seek to be called 'good girl' and 'good boy'. The children who become upset if they displease their adults.

Autistic children don't do those things. In their natural state, they could not care less about pleasing an adult, or anybody else as a matter of fact. They do nothing for the sake of earning praise. They don't give a damn if they displease somebody. Their message is as clear as the wind: they didn't ask to be brought into this world. They did not choose their parents or anything else about this life. From wherever they come, they act as if they've been kidnapped and brought here at a wrong time and into a wrong place. So now deal with it.

And yet many autistic children will participate in the functioning of this world to a certain extent – although it may be an extent that makes sense to them and maybe to them only. Eating food (a restricted list of foods, certainly) is one thing sure to make sense. Everything else may be open to question. I know of children for whom sleeping does not make sense; they would rather stay awake all the time. I know of children for whom time not spent in motion is wasted.

And when reality does not make sense to them, when they are being pulled out of their inner world for a purpose that does not appeal to them, autistic children react painfully.

And yet, they can be trained.

ChOT is an illusion that serves to trick the mind of the autistic child (as well as anybody else's, by the way). It allows the child's (or other person's) mind to treat the reality – that he *must* act in a certain way – not as enforcement ("NO!!!") but as an invitation to exercise personal will-power ("I choose this").

When we force an autistic child to shift attention from the comfort of the hidden reality of his/her mind and interact with the civilized world, ChOT serves two purposes:

1. It gives the child an opportunity to exercise will (by preserving the sense of inner freedom, which seems to be very important whether or not one is autistic).

2. It gives the child an opportunity to protest against the external world (by rejecting at least half of the offered choices).

ChOT gives the child an opportunity to REJECT; and the child really needs this opportunity.

In some Japanese factories, it is customary to have a plastic dummy of the boss set up in a place where workers can hit it. ChOT may have an analogous effect on the autistic child's psyche. The mere possibility of expressing protest offers healing and reduces stress.

All of these thoughts came to me as I watched Billy's reactions to ChOT. His reactions were a testimony about how hard life on Earth is for him. I sensed that often he feels as if enclosed in a room where the walls are full of sharp objects. He tries to find an exit, but instead he hits the walls, and it hurts. He knows he's been told many times how to find the exit. But he can't remember. He gets nervous. He hits the walls more and more. Soon his mind is all bruises. It hurts all over. And he throws himself on the floor and screams as hard as his lungs let him. He is asking to be taken out. He screams for help. Except he does not remember the word "help." He does not remember anything. He is just plain scared of this room with its sharp objects.

Is anybody out there?

When organizing in your mind the choices to be offered, think of several choices that would be easy and fun to reject. The purpose is to give the child chances to exercise his/her need to PROTEST and REJECT to the greatest extent possible.

Once the need to reject reality is satisfied, the child will go for that one choice which he least objects to. He will take a bath. He will go to bed. He will eat the cereal.

He will have no tantrum.

We've used ChOT in many ways. ChOT helped tremendously in getting Billy to talk and in building his vocabulary.

For example: I show Billy two cups. I pour juice into them, one full and one half. Then I say several times, pointing my finger at the cups, "Half cup." "Full cup." By this time Billy is ready for a drink. I try to make him say the word "half" or "full" before I give him a cup. He always wants the full one, even though he usually drinks only half of it.

It took several weeks of this exercise before we had our first success in imposing a new word on Billy. He said the word "full."

Very soon I was just asking, "Full cup or half cup?" without pouring juice into two cups or pointing a finger. "Full cup!" he'd answer.

We wasted a lot of juice for the sake of his learning to speak. We had juice-drinking several times a day, and every time I made Billy say "full cup," he said it better and with more ease.

At some point, when Billy was seven, I finally changed the routine to, "How about if I give you half cup, and if you want more, I will give you more when you're done." And he was OK with it.

I will give some examples of dialogs that I've used with Billy. When I first began using ChOT, I had to think in advance about the options I'd give him. Options began to haunt my thoughts. Thinking of options helped me to be more creative, and in the end, more spontaneous in using ChOT.

- Which towel would you like, the small one, the one with squares, or this one that's huge and soft? (After a few weeks Billy learned how to say "huge and soft.")

- Which flavor of toothpaste would you like: baking soda, garlic, or bubble gum? (The answer is obvious.)

- Would you like a plain cold bath, a cold bath with floating ice, or a lovely warm bath?

- Would you like boiled macaroni or fried macaroni?

- Do you want your sandwich cut in two, four or six pieces? (Over the years we had periods in which he opted for different numbers of pieces. For one period of several months, Billy was very particular about getting the right number of pieces, mostly four. More recently, he is asking to have the whole sandwich, uncut. I can see how satisfying it is to him to reject all the choices we've offered him in the past and, instead, to come up with his own choice.)

- How many books do you want to take in the car: two small books, one medium book, or four big books?

- Do you want one chicken leg, two chicken legs or some yummy smoked fish?

- Do you want a plate, or your favorite blue bowl?

- Do you want one kiss, two kisses, or no kiss at all?

- Do you want a hug now or after dinner, or both?

- Do you want to feel grumpy for five minutes, ten minutes, or fifteen minutes?

- Do you want us to go to the car holding hands, or do you want to walk by yourself?

And so on. I try to offer options in a way that one seems much more attractive to Billy than the others. In some of the examples above, Billy's view of attractiveness may differ from what you would expect. For instance, the choice of kisses was offered when he disliked what I was telling him to do, and he relished the opportunity to say haughtily, "No kiss at all!" It gave him immediate emotional satisfaction, and possibly eliminated a future tantrum.

The creative use of ChOT can actually be enjoyable. Billy and I both like it. And, as happened in my case, the habit of offering choices may drift beyond your autistic child and become a sensible and gentle way to deal with other people too.

19

Dealing with Physical Sensitivities

Billy, like many autistic children, is very sensitive physically – very "touchy." My skin seems to have the sensitivity of cowhide compared to his. Compared to Billy, I can endure a range of temperatures that would make me seem, to him, a combination of a polar bear and a lizard.

Tags

Billy's biggest sensitivity is to tags in clothing.

I used to tolerate tags. My clothes aged with the neck tags still sewn in. Those little neck tags with the names of famous designers – or even just GAP – are a silent confirmation of one's status. Clothes need neck tags. Or so I thought.

Not anymore. Not since I realized that the reason for the tantrum Billy was having was a neck tag.

It was a nice neck tag. It said "Eddie Bauer," and it made me feel good. I was proud to have my boy have it next to his neck. When I realized that simply cutting it off could stop the tantrum, I chopped it right off.

From then on, whenever we bought some new article of clothing for Billy, I made sure to cut off all the tags immediately. And if I happened to forget, Billy was sure to remind me the first time he put on the clothing.

We have a tag-free life now. Eventually I started to cut the tags from Francesca's clothing too, as if leaving them on might mean that I didn't care as much about her skin as I cared about Billy's. And at some point I realized that I was starting to be bothered by some of the tags on my own clothes too. So off they went.

We wouldn't be able to trace the makers of a lot of our clothes these days. But we find them more comfortable.

Weather

Another of Billy's major sensitivities is weather – or more specifically, cold.

When we moved from New York City to San Diego, our decision to move was not based on Billy's sensitivity to weather. At the time we were deciding to move, we actually hadn't realized yet (we'd had only three winters to figure it out, after all) that many of the tantrums which we had endured were weather-related. We did figure it out before we actually moved; and this realization sped us on our way to Southern California.

In Connecticut, the winters when Billy was one and two, he was unpleasant and tempestuous; but he didn't spend a lot of time outdoors, and we drove him in a warm car, and he wasn't big enough to be an impossible handful between house and car or car and store. In New York City the next year, getting about by public transportation or on foot, at age three he was an impossible two hands full.

Billy hated the cold. He hated the wind. He hated the sleet and the snow blowing into his face. He hated being wet. He hated his fingers trapped in mittens, but he also hated his fingers being chilled outside the mittens. He hated being confined for long hours inside, but he couldn't make himself happy in the cold outside.

During the cold months, Billy had severe tantrums every morning when he had to leave our apartment building. He just didn't want to go out. We had to drag him out. We had to force his little body out of the building. And then he'd throw himself on the ground, refusing to move. So we'd have to carry him. And he was heavy. And he opposed being carried. And people looked at us, shaking their heads. I recognized the look in their eyes. It was the look of people who would never allow *their* kid to behave like that.

When we figured out that the weather had a major impact on Billy's behavior, we came up with some partial solutions.

Even though Billy was older than three and already out of a stroller, I found a large, sturdy stroller which could shelter even a big boy like him. We put him in the stroller before we left the building, making sure that he was wrapped in a soft blanket big enough that he could hide under it, head and hands and all.

If we were taking the car, I warmed up the car before taking Billy to it.

I took him to playrooms and to McDonald's to play.

We endured.

But the real solution to the weather tantrums was San Diego. This city was the proving ground for God when designing the weather for Heaven. It is such a blessing to have this bountiful sunshine and to have it almost every day.

Once in a while my husband and I become nostalgic for the wilder forces of nature. I think of snowfalls in Moscow and days so cold that the snow plays a violin under your feet as you walk. And my husband longs for a good Nebraska thunderstorm.

But our nostalgia doesn't last long. Seeing Billy happily running from the house to the back yard and back into the house and out again, and not having to worry about his reaction to the weather, brings us back to thanking God for San Diego.

One day I will spread my wings and I will fly to Moscow on a winter day. And there I'll take the train to that park just outside the city where twenty-some years ago I used to jog barefoot in the snow with a small group of fellow enthusiasts and swim in an ice hole in the park's small lake. And I will swim in the cold water and it will feel so good. And then I will spread my wings again and I will fly back to San Diego.

Sensory helpers

Brushing

After Billy was diagnosed as autistic, the San Diego School District assigned him an occupational therapist. She introduced us to brushing as a means of reducing Billy's physical sensitivity. She brushed him all over with a small plastic brush. Whole-body brushing is said to be helpful for many autistic children. But it didn't do much for Billy.

An important issue connected with brushing, often overlooked in special-education classes, is whether the child accepts the procedure. When Billy was in kindergarten class, his occupational therapist, speech therapist and teacher were all different than in his preschool year. And while he developed a rapport with the speech therapist and the teacher, the occupational therapy sessions were consistently problematic. I went to observe a session, and I saw that Billy and his OT Lady didn't like each other very much.

Well, that was a problem. Billy was not comfortable letting himself be touched unless he liked the person doing the touching. And he didn't. I didn't feel that I could insist that he let himself be touched by a person he didn't like; and even if I had felt that I could insist, my insistence would not impress Billy. Not even if the touching person is an OT Lady. Not even if the brushing is officially prescribed in writing in his Individual Educational Plan

(IEP). So I asked to have the brushing procedure dropped from his OT sessions.

Privacy is also an issue not always considered in special-education classrooms. Brushing at school was done in a room full of people. A special-education class usually has a reduced number of students – eight to fourteen in Billy's classes. But that does not mean that the classroom is not crowded. There are teacher's aides, personal aides (assistants who are assigned to work with only one specific child), speech therapists, occupational therapists. Sometimes a small class ends up having more people than the room can comfortably accommodate.

Would you like to have your skin brushed in a place where there's no privacy whatsoever? Would you be able to relax, and enjoy it, and let it reduce your sensory deficiencies?

I've seen children being brushed outside of their classroom while at the same time other children were running wild around them. I've seen kids being brushed through clothes made of synthetic fabrics (can you imagine the static effect?).

Brushing at the school, as I observed it, was reduced to a mechanical procedure done just to fulfill a requirement of a child's IEP. It was not a warm or relaxing experience.

Massage

Billy had always liked a massage. I believed that he responded to my hands because they are warm and soft, gentle and loving. It seemed no wonder that he would rather be massaged by my hands than by a brush. The brushes which I've seen occupational therapists use are plastic. They don't seem to me to be very soft and comforting, and I don't think Billy found them so either.

As an experiment, I went shopping and bought a fancy duster made of soft lambswool. Then I found a bunch of wonderfully soft fur toys in a pet store. I brushed Billy with the duster and those fur toys. I rubbed his back with the duster. He loved to stick some of the fur toys under his shirt. He'd keep them in his bed and carry them in the car.

So I brushed Billy at home. I brushed him with soft fur brushes, which were very personal because I brought them to him as surprise gifts. I brushed him in a quiet place at a quiet time. I made sure to have plenty of time so that I could honor as many "mores" and "here, toos" as he could come up with. I liked brushing him at night so that he could let himself be brushed into the dream world. At that time I felt like a powerful magician who could, with gentle strokes of a duster, manufacture happiness.

20

Reserves of Body and Soul

I've learned the hard way how important it is to be aware of the inner reserves I have available to devote to Billy's training, what I call "Reserves of Body and Soul," but from now on I'll just call them "Reserves." It's important not only to be aware of them, but also to be able to continuously assess how much of my Reserves I'm spending throughout the day, and in what ways I'm spending them. This knowledge is an indispensable tool in parenting an autistic child.

Early on, I realized that my ability not only to get Billy through the day, but also to help him in a constructive way, depended on the state of my own body and soul as much as on the state of his. I had to learn to assess and calibrate my daily needs of energy, both of body and soul. I had to learn to respect these needs and to honor them. I had to learn to build my life around them, not in spite them.

Our Reserves are not limitless. But many of us spend day after day as if our Reserves have no limit. Using up our Reserves eventually comes to haunt us. For me this haunting came in the form of depression, desperation, tearfulness and fatigue. I have found that it's easier not to overdraw my Reserves than to pay off an overdraft once it has been incurred.

I assess my average daily Reserves at one hundred points – an arbitrary number, but easy to work with. This is what I start with on an average morning. Note that this is a self-assessment – my judgment of how much I can do that day. Some days I may feel down, and my Reserves points could be less than a hundred to start with.

I expect to spend about twenty-five Reserves points on the morning routine, to make sure that both children have an organized and a happy and peaceful start to their day. I also keep track of the Battles in which I'm already engaged (about Battles, see Chapter 23) and try to keep in mind the number of points I will need to sustain those Battles. The children's homework takes about twenty Reserves points. A good day would be one in which I have some unused Reserves points left by 10 p.m., when I can claim a little of MY time.

There was a time of darkness in my life. That was the time before I got smart and started to assess my Reserves. During that time my Reserves were in perpetual deficit. I'd get up in the morning and take care of the children. I'd endure Billy's tantrums, and at some point I'd know I needed to find a quiet place to cry. After a cry, my soul felt cleaner, as if a gentle rain had washed it.

It is very important to accept that your Reserves of body and soul are limited, and to acknowledge that caring for an autistic child takes an enormous amount of energy. There is no comparison between parenting a typical child and parenting an autistic child.

Parenting an autistic child can be a rewarding experience, but it is a draining one. It helps to be able to evaluate your resources at any time of day and to be able to establish what amount of help and what kind of help you need in order to go through a day without being drained to a point at which you barely remember your own name.

You might ask, "Isn't it enough just to say: I'm tired, I need rest?"

Not in my experience. Counting your Reserves allows you not to get to the point where you have to admit you're exhausted. It allows you to predict, to some degree, how the day will go. And it helps preserve your dignity. It surely helped me with mine. Instead of an emotional display – "Don't you see how drained I am?" – it allowed me to state, in a quiet voice, "I've used 120 points so far." This statement tells my husband that he needs to take over. He knows I'm well over the limit and close to a breakdown – even if I seem to be as cool as a cucumber.

I prefer not to use emotional displays to make a point. I'd rather not be loud in order to be heard. I'd rather not moan in order to wake compassion in someone. I'd rather not show anger in order to make a message come through.

Well, I haven't mastered cool substitutes for all the emotional displays that are still a part of my life, which have their own meanings and respond to certain needs. But I'm at a good start. By trying to be always aware of my Reserves points, I've eliminated the majority of my emotional displays. And so can you.

The next time we meet, I may ask, "How are you?"

And you may smile and answer, "Oh, I've used 450 Reserves points in the last three days. Otherwise I'm perfectly fine."

And I will give you a hug from all my heart. I will pour you a glass of red Moldavian wine and spread some butter on a piece of fresh bread. We will drink and eat, and we will feel good. Because I will know how you feel. And you will know that I know. And there will be no need to say so.

21

Starting the Day

For a long time, I found it hard to start the day with Billy. Every day I felt like a soldier taken by surprise.

Before I had children, I used to exercise first thing every morning. Once upon a time I did yoga. At another time I jogged. I biked. I frequented a gym. I enjoyed all these enough that they were no test of my will-power.

But motherhood changed that. I stopped exercising; I was too sleepy in the morning and too tired the rest of the time. And although I acknowledged the need to move my muscles and attempted here and there to introduce some exercise into my schedule, I could maintain enthusiasm only for a little while.

I started to exercise again on a regular basis only when Billy was six, when I started to train him using behavior modification.

One of the first things we worked on was his morning schedule. I needed to train him to do the routine procedures – washing, dressing, and so on. And although training was a taxing endeavor, there was another aspect of the morning which was also difficult, maybe even more so. That aspect was waking up to an autistic boy.

When Billy awoke, he usually was still carrying the spirit of an animal from his book or movie of the evening before. One morning he'd jump from the bed on his hands and knees and bark. He was a dog. Another morning he'd make weird animal sounds and roll on the floor, and I'd realize that I was dealing with the seal from yesterday's cartoon. Billy could perfectly impersonate whatever creature had captured his body, mind, and spirit. The problem was that the creature had power over Billy and I didn't. That creature had so much power that it left no room for me to enter his space and direct him into the activities of a human's morning. Billy did not feel like a human. He was SEAL, and seals do not brush their teeth or put on clothes.

Breaking through Billy's impersonations was the hardest part. Once a crack opened in the impersonation, the morning routine rolled more or less smoothly. I spent great emotional effort to create that crack.

When the alarm clock or Billy brought me out of my dreams and my eyes opened, merciless reality invaded my consciousness: yet another day of struggle with autism. That invasion made me feel sorry for myself. Like most people, I enjoy feeling sorry for myself, of course; but only for a short time. When it happens day after day, bells begin ringing in my ears telling me it's time to do something.

At that time I started taking a walk in the morning before anyone else in the family woke up. At this stage Billy had begun getting up at six, so I had to get up at five to complete my walk before he awoke. I started walking not for my physical benefit, but to prepare myself for encountering Billy.

During my morning walk I said my prayers. I asked God to fill my soul with faith and understanding, with strength and tolerance, with firmness and tenderness. I mentally rehearsed my interactions with Billy. I rehearsed a strong voice, kind eyes, a soft and comforting body language. I asked God to stay close to me through the day, to witness me, and back me up. I had several short prayers, and I repeated them ten times each using my fingers to keep track of the counting. I thought of getting myself a string with ten beads on it, but I never got around to that.

I was barely done with all my prayers by the time my forty-five-minute walk was over. But I came home a different person. I didn't feel invaded anymore. Reality was not taking charge of me. I was taking charge of reality.

If it was a morning when Billy was Seal, I'd approach him in a very gentle way. "Hi, little seal! Good morning, little seal!"

"I'm not a seal!" Billy would react.

"Oh yes, I think you are. You're making the sounds of a seal, and you look to me like a seal, too. A cute one."

"No! I'm your son Billy!"

"Are you? How come you talk so funny?"

"Mom…"

"Are you sure you're not a seal and your name is not Little Iceball?"

"No, Mom! I said I'm your son Billy!"

"Well, but if you're my Billy, then you must be a boy."

"I *am* a boy!"

"But boys brush their teeth and put on their clothes in the morning."

"Yeah, *I* know."

At this point Billy was very amusing. He sounded defeated and sad. He faced a human reality that seemed harsh to him, yet he knew he had got himself into it with his own little hands.

I knew I'd still have to deal with getting him through his morning wake-up schedule (see Chapter 16); but I'd made a crack in his animal impersonation, and that meant that more than half of the morning's work was done.

Now, two years later, Billy still often wakes up as a prisoner of some spirit or another. These days the spirits are mostly dragons, or knights, or Gandalf. I like it when he is being Gandalf, walking with his back bent over a stick, although he sings the Orc song, "Where there's a whip, there's a way." Billy's transitions from the spirit-guest to his own sweet self are much easier than they used to be. He can actually joke about his need to impersonate. If he's a dragon, I can tell him that his breath stinks of ashes and he'd better brush his teeth. Billy loves it when I participate in his dramas.

And I still get myself up at five and out of the house every single morning, even if I've gone to bed well after midnight, because I know I can manage to catch up on sleep, but if I'm not prepared to take charge of reality the first thing in the morning, reality will take charge of me. And who knows where it would take me? I surely don't want to find out.

22

Organizing the Struggle

My husband and I don't always agree on how to manage Billy. We sometimes change places in being "the good guy" and "the bad guy." We both drift from generosity to ridiculous impatience. And yes, we even point fingers at one another. At least, he does. Not me.

But we get better at choosing our fights with each other and with Billy. Actually, my husband and I haven't had any good fights for quite a long time. Now we have friendly discussions. We have campaigns. We have goals and achievements.

If the extent of our disagreements were compared to rainfall, then we've moved from Oregon to Arizona. It did not happen overnight, and it did not happen by itself. We worked at it, Bill and I.

He did his part by standing like a rock. Whatever happened, storm or no storm, he stood there.

Bill is a prairie man, a man of few words, not free with signs of affection. Stubborn when it comes to preserving the things he values. Family is one of them. We can always count on his standing straight for us. That is his part, and it's a powerful one.

And I'm the one who is on the move. I will run to the end of the world if there is promise of a miracle. I am the one who knocks on doors and asks for help. I am the one to shed tears. To melt in affection. To be desperate. To be blessed with answers. To repent. To be forgiven. To rejoice and to bow.

And so it may not come as a surprise that we've had differences about handling Billy.

I remember Billy's preschool year, when he was in Theresa's class. A school bus took Billy to school and brought him home. The boy did not mind the bus. He was actually excited about it. At the beginning it was the excitement of the newness of the event. Then it was the excitement of meeting Chris every morning. Chris was six years older and was Billy's only contact with "big boys."

Every morning we went through a regular cycle of tantrums before Billy was ready for school. These included getting him to open his eyes, fishing him from under his blanket, chasing him when he tried to escape to our bedroom, fishing him from under *our* blanket, and getting him through the bathroom routine, through dressing and through eating.

By the end of this pilgrimage, Billy was often ready and glad to go out of the house and meet Chris and the bus.

Not always, though. Sometimes he'd sit on the pavement and refuse to walk to the bus stop. Sometimes he didn't want to get on the bus. And then Chris transferred to another school, and it was only Billy waiting for the bus, and he missed his companion.

Winter in San Diego is not like winter in New York City, but on some mornings it may get chilly. We don't wear boots or parkas in San Diego. The same sweater serves year around. So I guessed that if I could make Billy more comfortable on those chilly mornings, he would cope better with the transition between home and the school bus.

On days when I took Billy to the bus stop, I would get out of the house a little bit earlier than we had to. I took a light blanket with me, and at the bus stop I sat on the sidewalk, wrapped Billy in the blanket, held him on my lap and tried to be sweet. He loved it. I loved it. I was sure it was helping with the transition.

But I had a problem with big Bill.

He did not think it was proper for me to baby a four-year-old boy, especially out in the open, in full view of the whole neighborhood. We had a disagreement, and at that time we didn't yet have a protocol for solving our disagreements. The protocol came later.

So I tried to get away with my way. Instead of carrying a blanket, I'd put on a large sweater and use it as a blanket when Billy and I were out of my husband's sight. When Bill took Billy to the bus stop, I'd stay home and suffer.

Then the spring came and the mornings became warmer. Things got better.

Later, Bill and I developed a protocol for solving our disagreements about Billy. The last step in our protocol is Theresa. We chose her as our arbitration court. When it becomes clear that Bill and I stand in different worlds and these worlds are not moving toward each other, I call Theresa.

It was at a later arbitration meeting with Theresa that the question of providing Billy with comfort came up. And Theresa told us a story.

Shortly before that, Theresa had taken it upon herself to foster a child from her special-ed preschool class. R was a boy whose mother had not managed to make good choices for her children. While the system tried to sort out legal and parenting rights, R had the good fortune to live with Theresa.

Theresa shared with us the story of her morning routines as a foster mother. The number and intensity of the struggles she had to fit between 6:30 a.m. and 7:30 a.m. were very familiar to us – all the obstacles, the failures, and the victories. She also told us how important sensory comfort was for her boy. She would put the boy's clothes in the dryer and take them out one by one as she dressed him, so that they all felt warm and comforting. When it was time to drive R to school, before she took him out of the house she would wrap him in a warm blanket and carry him, wrapped, to the car. There she strapped the safety belt around the boy and the blanket. The warmth helped the boy cope with the day. And every little bit of help counts.

After that conversation I felt fully justified in ironing every piece of Billy's clothes in the morning as he put them on. He'd stand right next to the ironing board and utter a sigh of pleasure every time his little body felt the warmth of another piece of clothing. For me, this process became the high point of the morning. Amidst an avalanche of grouchy reactions, I could actually witness pleasure and gratitude, expressed in such a sweet way. It was worth any amount of trouble.

Later I learned to use my hair dryer to warm Billy's clothes by blowing them full of warm air. Now Billy is eight, and we still sometimes warm up his clothes, although not as often as before. But it is surely a good tool to calm a boy on a morning that is threatening to turn tumultuous.

23

The Warrior-Parent

I don't like the word "fights." To me, fights are impulsive and emotional encounters with no structure to them, no organization. I like the word "Battles," with a capital B. Battles remind me of generals and admirals. They remind me of smart, cool-headed men who are determined to win, men with a strategic plan, who design clever tactics. When they go into a Battle they do it without screaming or crying. They do it with dignity.

One day I set that as a goal for myself. I set out to find a way to raise my autistic boy with dignity. To be like an admiral serving a noble cause. I set out to choose only those Battles which I believed I could win.

It is important to understand that a series of reminders does not add up to a Battle. Serial reminders ("chaotic reminders," I prefer to call them) may work with typical children – sometimes. With autistic children, chaotic reminders do not work. Forget them.

It's pretty much as with dogs. You can't remind a dog to go outside for his private needs. He won't do it unless you train him. It is this training process that I call a Battle. The Battle (training process) has three elements:

1. a clear goal
2. a realistic plan to achieve the goal
3. realistic time limits.

You may choose to remind an autistic child to stop shaking, or making noise, or smearing food on the table, or chewing on clothes. It is not likely that this will cause the child to stop the behavior. The probability is quite high that mounting reminders that do not bring the desired response from the child will result in a neurotic response in the adult. Which quite probably will trigger a neurotic reaction in the child.

I've experienced this chain of reactions myself, more times than I care to admit. Whenever this happened, I suffered, because it bothers me to act without dignity. For me, it became easier to plan and sustain a Battle than to suffer. And although proficiency in choosing and conducting battles ultimately helped my sense of dignity, it also helped me to preserve energy, sleep better, and be happier altogether.

Choosing a Battle is a seven-step process.

1. *Recognize which situations can be improved by battling them, and which can't.*

2. *Assess your enemy.*

3. *Weigh the power distribution.* Decide if the Battle is worthwhile and if you have enough determination to fight it to the end.

4. *Calculate your Reserves.* Do you have enough to dedicate to this Battle daily? Make sure you continue to track all the Battles in which you are engaged. Assess how many Reserves points you need for the new Battle, and compare it with the balance of your Reserves points.

5. *Make a plan for the Battle.* Rehearse the plan in your mind.

6. *Prepare any materials that may assist you.*

7. *Decide on D-Day.* Put it in the calendar. *Wish yourself luck.*

Whether or not you decide to undertake a particular Battle, you should in any event make a conscious decision to *stop using chaotic reminders.*

Chaotic reminders are like random shooting at the front lines. At the front, soldiers don't shoot at random. They might kill someone from their own side. Shooting is a part of a deliberate plan, and it has a definite direction to it. Reminders usually are not and do not.

Some random shooting:

- "How many times have I told you!!!!"

- "Not again!!!"

- "Can't you understand when I say it over and over???"

- "Don't keep on [*insert a disagreeable action in which the child is engaged*]!!!"

These profound statements have an established position in the vocabularies of more than a few parents. I've heard them in Russian. I've heard them in Romanian. My children can understand them only in English, but even if I were to say them in Albanian, they'd get the drift. Helpless emotionalism transcends words and languages.

By giving up chaotic reminders and saving your efforts for Battles, you get away, little by little, from that helpless emotionalism.

You stop being a worrier-parent. You become a warrior-parent.

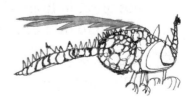

24

An Example of a Battle-Plan

Billy loves to snack while watching television. It happens that in front of our television set there is a beautiful, hand-made Oriental carpet. My husband went to great trouble to hand-carry that carpet from Kazakhstan, and now he wants to enjoy the crafts-manship that went into it.

Billy has not yet learned to appreciate the beauty of the carpet. He also has not yet learned to be a tidy eater. Which brings us to crumbs on the carpet. I leave it to you to guess the feelings which crumbs may arouse in the heart of a man who has hand-carried a carpet from Kazakhstan.

Now, it takes hard work to get Billy to do anything in any way other than the one he has in mind. When he has in mind a snack in front of the television, keeping him from it is a big job. To change Billy's behavior to his father's satisfaction would require 1. to stop him from eating in front of the television, or 2. to make him a tidy eater.

I think about the situation. This is my evaluation:

1. *Recognize the situation.* Billy could, in principle, be taught not to eat in front of the television. He also could be trained to be a tidy eater.

2. *Assess your enemy and your resources.* My enemy in getting Billy not to eat in front of the television would be his

determination to hold on to one of the main events of his day. He loves eating in front of the television. It is convenient. It makes him happy.

My resources in changing this habit are limited. There are very few alternatives that I could offer to compensate for the loss of eating in front of the television. The only major resource would be my will-power; but this would bring us to a clash of wills; and this is the worst way of getting into a Battle. I don't like to rely only on a clash of wills unless the situation is extremely important and there's nothing else to be done.

In getting Billy to be a tidy eater, my enemy would be his very limited awareness of his body. To engage in a Battle to build his awareness is inconceivable to me at the moment. I don't have the resources.

3. *Assess the distribution of power.* The power distribution is unfavorable. Billy is ready to defend his habit with all his might. I lack determination. (After all, I'm not the one who carried the carpet from Kazakhstan.)

4. *Calculate your Reserves.* I would need a minimum of twenty Reserves points a day, throughout the Battle, to train Billy in new habits. I would need to come up with some stories to demonstrate to him that what we, his parents, are asking of him actually makes sense. At this point it doesn't really make sense to Billy to give up eating in front of the television. I don't have twenty extra Reserves points. If I start battling Billy on this front, I would put myself onto the negative side on my Reserves scale.

Conclusion: I don't need to go on to consider points 5 through 7. It's pointless to start this Battle. I know I won't win.

Is there anything to do but admit defeat? Maybe.

I offer to my husband to put the carpet into the attic until Billy gets bigger and learns better habits. This proposal is not accepted.

So I think again. I come up with following proposal: 1. we allow Billy to eat in front of the television, but only if he locates himself not on the carpet but on the bricks in front of the fireplace; or 2. we allow Billy to eat in front of the television if there is a blanket on top of the carpet.

I would have to make sure that, every time Billy eats in front of the television, either he locates himself on the bricks or he (or someone) brings a blanket and spreads it on the carpet. And I (or someone) would have to make sure that Billy learns the new rules for eating in front of the television: bricks or blanket.

This is an easy Battle. Billy will comply with the new rules because he still gets to eat in front of the television. The distribution of power is now favorable, and I (or someone) won't have to use up many Reserves points.

But it may take several months before Billy's awareness is raised to a point at which he automatically settles himself on the bricks or asks for a blanket. So for that time the responsibility for his awareness is on someone else. "Someone else" means me – or my husband.

My husband goes along with my proposal. We agree to share the responsibility for Billy's awareness.

We shake hands.

Love is grand.

25

Another Battle Considered

When my children take off their socks, the socks end up inside out. The children leave these dirty socks wherever they happen to take them off.

I went through several stages in dealing with this situation.

At first I succumbed to the habit of chaotic reminders. I'd find socks in odd places around the house, and I'd let myself be upset. I felt unappreciated, or at least underappreciated. I clean, I do the laundry, I sort out and stock nicely paired clean socks for my children. All I ask is for them to take their socks off right side out and to throw them into the laundry basket. It's so easy! Why can't they do such a simple thing for my sake?

The next stage was the one in which I realized that 1. my reminders were not bringing success and 2. I had issued so many reminders that I felt undignified issuing any more.

So I contemplated a Battle.

1. *The situation.* Since both children were habitual
    sock-laundry abusers, the Battle would be to change a
    habit in both of them. I'd have to wash some of their
    dirty socks inside out and some of them right side out.
    Then I'd have to show them the difference – that indeed
    socks get cleaner if they are washed right side out.

2. *The enemy.* Such a demonstration, plus some encouragement along the way, might be enough to instill a new habit in Francesca. It would not affect Billy. Billy would need more elaborate training. I would have to make an effort to be present every time he takes off his socks. I'd need to come up with a little song to help him with the building of a new habit. Something like, "As I help my socks go down, go down, I wish them a lovely trip to the laundry town, laundry town." I'll have to work on the lyrics.

3. *The distribution of power.* The children's power comes from two places: their ingrained habits, and their laziness. If I'm convinced that the cause is important and necessary, I can draw enough power from my conviction to win the Battle. But I don't have that conviction about the sock problem.

4. *Reserves.* I'd need about five to seven points daily. (This is purely subjective, but based on my experience.) That's not a lot; but the daily average of my leftover points, after I fight the Battles already in progress, is about ten points. With this balance available I can spend some time with my husband or read a book after the children go to bed. I've learned that it is not a good idea to spend all my Reserves points on the children. If I reach exhaustion, something in me starts becoming bitter. Some uninterrupted time by myself has a healing effect, even if it lasts only for thirty minutes. I can say a prayer or watch television, or take a bath, or drink a cup of tea. It is MY time. I own it.

Conclusion: The sock issue is not important enough for me to give up any of my free Reserves points. I can go on and collect the socks and throw them into the laundry myself. This is much easier than coming up with a training plan and enforcing it.

And in general it's not that big a deal. If the children grow up still leaving their dirty socks inside out, their social and professional lives will probably not be affected by it.

So I gave up the idea of a Sock-Battle. And of course I had to promise myself that I'd stop reminding the children to take care of their socks the way I want them to. The socks would become my job, my responsibility. I could do a good job and be proud of myself.

But the chaotic reminders would not help my pride, so they had to cease. I gave them up.

26

Some Battles in Progress

With Francesca we currently are working on the following issues:

- her table manners
- her magic words (please, thank you...)
- her homework schedule
- her music schedule
- whining
- her treatment of her brother.

With Billy, there are the following:

- the Battle to substitute, in place of noises, "words, and poems, and songs" (see Chapter 34)
- his writing
- his vocabulary
- his magic words
- his habit of touching people, whether or not he knows them
- his treatment of his sister
- his table manners

- his tendency to be loud and obnoxious
- tantrum prevention

For each of these Battles we have a plan. Some of the plans are more structured than others. The main thing is to carry on each Battle in a way which is constructive rather than draining. Both my husband and I participate in carrying on these Battles.

We started to be consistent with our Battles about two years ago. We can count some successes with Francesca, who is a "typical" child (that is, she is unique in a typical way).

- She whines substantially less now than a year or two ago.
- She has learned many ways in which she can be of support to her brother.
- She can abide by a schedule as long as we remind her to write one down.
- Her table manners have improved.

We have also made substantial progress with Billy.

- He has learned how and where to use the potty.
- He has learned to express his needs with words.
- He has reduced the amount of unintelligible noise he makes at least by half during the last year.
- When he drinks from a regular cup (as opposed to a lidded one), he spills only every other time.
- He has developed a loving attitude to his sister.
- At school the girls used to complain that he was hitting them; now they complain that he is kissing them.
- He is polite, rarely missing the magic words.
- He dresses and undresses by himself.

- He goes to bed easily.
- His morning routine has changed from misery to challenge.

And this all within only two years!

27

Autism and the Phases of the Moon

When I was growing up in the USSR, "religion" was a bad word. So were the words "Christ" and "Christmas." The authorities decreed that the human need for celebration would be satisfied exclusively by holidays inspired by 1. the Revolution, or 2. the coming of the New Year.

Revolutionary holidays had their State-prescribed (and State-organized) rituals – the tanks parading in Red Square on November 7, the workers marching on May Day – but because the changing of the year was free of ideological impact and of religious content, the people were allowed to celebrate New Year's Eve freely. And they did. The New Year's Eve celebration had no ideological stiffness to it. No one had to wonder if there had been enough praise for the Revolution at the dinner table. It was the merriest night of all, a night when the children could stay up as late as they chose. It had its own rituals, of course – this was Russia, after all – but they were not ordained by the State. They were old, and they were far more elaborate than American ideas of how to meet the New Year.

Americans use up all their winter celebratory zeal on Christmas. By the time New Year's Eve comes, enthusiasm blooms only in the hearts of devoted drinkers, who celebrate Bacchus along with the new number on the calendar.

That's too simple for my Russian soul.

Missing my old days, I've taken to celebrating New Year's Eve with American friends but in the Russian style. We gather about nine in the evening for dinner. Each person at the table gets a turn to speak about the year which is about to vanish – what it meant, what there was to be thankful for. We say a toast to the old year and leave the table without eating dessert.

It's time for our mutual concert. Everyone performs, entertaining the whole group to the best of his or her ability, and no one is left without a prize.

We listen to music and we dance.

At about 11:30 we return to the table, where each of us writes, in private, his or her wishes for the year to come. At midnight we raise a glass of champagne or sparkling apple cider and drink to the arrival of the new year. Then we put all our wishes into an old steel pot which, in Russia, I used for making corn meal. It's one of the few possessions remaining from my life there.

My husband sets fire to the wishes, and they burn to ashes.

Then we eat our dessert. As the sweetness dissolves into our souls, the wishes have taken on a life of their own. Written down and burned before witnesses, they cannot be retrieved or canceled. They're off onto the path of coming true.

The next day, when the infant year is just starting to awaken in cradle-calendars hanging on new-year walls, my husband goes to the very end of Point Loma, where a lighthouse stands high above the ocean. There is always wind there. And he looses the ashes of our desires into the wind. I think that, among the roads which lead to God, the one that starts at the lighthouse is a sure shortcut.

Billy loves our New Year's celebrations. He works hard in preparing his part in the concert. But this is not the reason I told you this story.

The reason for the story is to tell you about what I said as we were sitting at the dinner table when my turn came to talk about the passing of the year 1999 and what it had meant to me.

I said that it had been a great year for me, 1999, and that I was grateful to it for many things – but most of all I was grateful for having pre-menstrual syndrome (PMS).

My friends laughed, I guess because they thought it was funny. And in way, it was. But in another way, I was completely serious.

Understanding PMS gave me a clue to begin to understand my own mind, and then Billy's.

Many women are familiar with PMS, of course. More women are familiar with it than want to be. It may take a variety of forms, and at different times it may affect us in different degrees. There are physical symptoms such as pains or cramps. These are easy enough to deal with; they are of no interest to us. We are after the heart and after the soul. We are after the implications of PMS at the subtle level of feelings, those which are out of reach of such powers as Tylenol and Advil.

For most of my life, my periods have been nothing but a nuisance, a payment for womanhood and for the gift of having children. They were a function of the womb and had nothing to do with my brain. I took myself equally seriously whether I menstruated or not, and I expected others to do the same.

So when, one day, I told my husband that I wanted "to talk about us," and he refused on the account of my "being unreasonable because of your PMS," I didn't believe him. I was hurt. He invited me to recall how the times that I wanted "to talk about us" tended to coincide with my menstrual cycle. I found this mocking, to say the least. I insisted on defending my intellectual independence from the mere functioning of a gynecological organ. He didn't want to participate in the argument. My outrage skyrocketed. To have my feelings reduced to a monthly condition…!

Would a good-hearted man ever suggest anything like that? No! No! And again no! How could he not see that my words to him were a part of a Quest for Marital Truth? That I was emotionally elevated only because of his lack of cooperation in that Quest?

Four years have passed since then. My PMS has subsided. But, as you will see, it served a purpose. I'm very grateful for having had to suffer through it.

The moon goes around the sky, changing its shape, making sure that the women of the world menstruate on time.

On some days, getting up in the morning, I'd be overly sensitive to everything around me, and irritable too. Things which on the regular basis would not have affected me much – long queues at a cash register, spilled coffee, kids talking back – would suddenly stir waves of indignation, of sadness, of helplessness.

On those days the world, hour by hour, became a scary and unfriendly place. Life became too heavy to bear. And several hours into the condition it was clear that all the fault was (whose do you think?) my husband's.

Let's be fair. My husband, although as good a man as they come, is no angel. He is, of course, not gentle enough, not affectionate enough, and not other things enough. He has not read *Women Are From Mars, Men Are From Venus* (or whatever that book is called). He doesn't even know which aisle in our bookstore has the relationships books. This year he gave me a wonderful gift on my birthday but forgot the flowers. Obviously, no angel.

On most days this conclusion means close to nothing. But suddenly, when the moon and I came to connect in a way which made my soul vibrate with the intensity of a Mahler symphony, the fact that my husband was no angel became unbearable.

Tearful and desperate, I felt that I had to talk to my husband, that I had to make him "understand." But of course he didn't "understand." He was annoyed. He wished he could escape me, and he didn't make any effort to hide how he felt. He was, clearly, insensitive, which only proved further that he was wrong and I was right.

At that point I would start engaging in the use of what I call "limitless terms." That is when the parties in an argument use the words "always," "never," "ever," "forever," "nothing," "everything," "nowhere," "everywhere," "nobody," "everybody."

It was the realization that I was using these words that made me eventually start doubting whether my Quests for Marital Truth had an independent intellectual basis.

Eventually I had to admit to myself that it was the moon that was bringing my soul into its Mahlerian state of passion. I had to admit it to myself because, after the PMS was over, I could justify all my elevated emotions and rhetorical excursions but one. I could not justify my use of limitless terms.

It was long ago, back in the USSR, when I noticed how often people use limitless terms in arguments. "You always ignore me!" "You never hear a word I'm saying!" I was struck by the foolishness of using these words. Since all of us have limits, how could we claim that anything we do could be limitless?

The realization that I was using limitless terms made me accept that I was somewhat out of self-control during certain phases of the moon. Could it be that my husband was right?

I thought about it. I analyzed how I felt. I realized what could help me. At a sober point in the month, I approached my husband and explained to him how he could help. What I asked was of Gargantuan dimensions, but he agreed to try to help me. And it worked.

To start with, I imagined that the brain is composed of innumerable chambers. All our experiences are sorted among the chambers of the brain just as information is sorted into files in computers. New chambers are formed as they are needed.

As the experiences are sorted out, they are stored together with their emotional attachments. The emotions which were part of an experience become its emotional attachments in the storage chamber in the brain.

When we are in control of our brain, we have a certain ability to choose the chambers to which we may turn our attention. For example, during a test we may choose not to think about a friend. Or we choose not to think about a scratch on the car during an engrossing movie.

Even on regular days though, days unaffected by the moon's phases, we are not totally in control of our attention. A young man who has no personal experience of PMS and who is known for outstanding self-control may find himself thinking about his girl-friend during a test. Or during a movie he may find his mind drifting to the scratch on the car, even though he'd really rather not think about it.

Usually there is certain elasticity in our ability to direct attention.

Think of a person's attention as being pulled in two directions. At one end is our will-power. At the other end is the magnetic power of the experiences stored in our brain. Once the experiences are stored, they become a part of a huge ongoing brain-cinema. Every chamber is a perpetual-motion machine engaged against all the other chambers in a permanent fight for attention.

It's not easy to avoid dwelling on our experiences. People have used religious and spiritual practices to gain the ability to control their attention so that the will-power directs the attention smoothly and gently into and out of any chamber of the brain, or (in the case of Zen masters) avoids all of them completely.

During my moon times there was no elasticity in my ability to direct my attention. I had no control over which chambers of my brain trapped my attention. I lacked the will-power to move my attention from negative experiences to positive ones.

By the release of some hormones, through certain chemical changes, or for whatever other reasons, the chambers which won my attention during my moon times were those having negative emotions attached to them.

Thus, during that low time of the month my mind would drift exclusively toward experiences which made me sad, upset, unsettled, or angry. After several hours of having my attention drift among chambers with negative emotional attachments, I became an emotionally negative person myself.

It was interesting that there was a strong need to justify my negative feelings: I needed a scapegoat.

This magnetic power that the negative part of my brain exerted over my attention would last for two or three days. Those days were extremely difficult. The negative emotions built up to a hysterical apogee and then went slowly away. It was as if a dragon came to create wrack and ruin and then, after satisfying himself, went off to rest for another month. I began to think of him as the Dragon of Negativity.

I realized that I was poorly equipped to fight and win a battle with this Dragon of Negativity.

I also realized that the situation was made much worse if I was argued with. I knew that every time my husband defended himself, or told me that I was wrong, or said that it was just PMS, the Dragon of Negativity roared with satisfaction and doubled his strength, quadrupled it, increased it tenfold.

I approached my husband with the following requests:

- No matter how unreasonable my words may seem, agree with everything I say (and here the use of the limitless term "everything" is justified).

- No matter how wrong I am, tell me that I'm right.

- Treat me as if I am a little child, with due affection and even with baby-talk.

- Do not mention PMS.

- Praise me.

His first reaction was, "That would be hard to do."

I knew that. I went on to explain that I was asking only for a trial effort. I asked to be treated like that on the first day of my Mahlerian state of mind for a total of three months. I acknowledged that I was asking for a big favor. But what if his cooperation indeed would cure me? What if this meant no more PMS?

My husband respects a reasonable mind. My request seemed reasonable enough to him. (Or perhaps the alternatives were so unpleasant that it seemed worth trying.)

So on the first day of the next PMS, he did what I asked. His responses to my edginess and tearfulness were, "Of course it's my fault that you feel this way. It's OK to cry. Yes."

I ought to say that God gave my husband very little acting talent. The words he chose were not eloquent by any means. Agreeable phrases did not come naturally to him. It was pure fakery, an absolutely obvious effort. And yet it worked! My edginess and tearfulness quickly subsided, dissipated into nowhere. Those agreeable words calmed the Dragon in me. They put him to sleep.

I was grateful to my husband.

What does this have to do with the craft of raising an autistic child?

One day Billy was working up a temper tantrum because I would let him watch only two television shows, while he wanted to watch three. I heard myself telling him that he was ungrateful, that two shows were plenty, that if he didn't stop crying, I would not let him watch any movie that night.

I heard myself saying those sensible words, and I realized that I was doing the same thing that my husband used to do during my PMS – being reasonable and stating truths to a person who is in distress and whose reactions to reality did not fit into the category "normal."

I was speaking reasonable words to a little boy whose attention was stuck in one chamber of his brain. By telling him that he was wrong, I only caused him to sink deeper and deeper into that chamber.

What I saw was that Billy, like me during my PMS, lacked the will-power to direct his attention. The Dragon of Negativity was somewhere inside him, and that Dragon had control of his attention. Billy, ruled by the Dragon, was determined to get what he wanted (television!), and to get it at all costs. At that moment, nothing else in the world existed for Billy. His attention had room for nothing but that burning desire to have his television show.

I realized that my little boy could not possibly fight that Dragon by himself. He needed help.

I went back to my own experience and analyzed it. And I concluded that there might not be much difference between Billy's tantrums and my disturbed emotions during PMS. If something helped me, maybe the same thing could help him.

I decided to treat it as unimportant that his distress had a different cause from mine. When I throw clothes into the laundry, the dirt on them may have a wide range of origins; yet one detergent cleans most of it.

So I needed a plan to 1. put to sleep the Dragon that was dominating his attention, and then 2. redirect the attention, preferably to a positive side of his brain.

I came up with OMAFED.

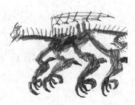

28

OMAFED

"OMAFED" is an acronym for "Open-Minded Assistance for the Emotionally Disturbed." It is a technique to head off emotional disturbances before they escalate out of control. "Buying time" (Chapter 14) is a technique that I use when a tantrum is already underway. OMAFED, used soon enough, keeps a tantrum from beginning.

OMAFED is based on the following observations:

1. Emotional distress awakens a Dragon of Negativity in a person.

2. This Dragon can rapidly grow to devastating size.

3. Certain reactions of the outside world to the person's emotional distress only feed the Dragon's growth. Among these reactions are reasonableness, righteousness, stating of truthful facts, and threats of any kind.

4. The Dragon of Negativity may be shrunk back to an egg by performing certain procedures.

Shrinking the Dragon

Step 1. Tell the person in distress that:

- he/she is absolutely right to feel the way he/she feels

- he/she has a right to feel that way.

Step 2. Show the person in distress a certain amount of compassion. Things to be emphasized:

- the person has a very hard life
- in a similar situation you'd feel much worse
- no tears are really enough to justify the sadness of the situation.

Step 3. When the distress starts to abate, suggest that something good might possibly happen.

Step 4. Show a way out. Propose something that will make up for the sadness; but make sure to keep on acknowledging that the sadness has a right to exist. The thing which you are proposing is meant not to deny sadness, but to bring some joy to offset it; so by all means do *not* suggest there's no point in feeling sad! Continue being compassionate.

Step 5. Enjoy a quick end to the tantrum. Feel good about having helped a soul.

29

Using OMAFED

The next time Billy got upset about my enforcement of the television rules, I tried my new plan of assistance, OMAFED.

I turned off the television. Billy's face instantly rearranged itself into a mask of a little samurai ready to fight to the very end for his lord. His lord was the Dragon that was keeping his attention focused exclusively on that missing show. And so I asked my Lord for help.

Then I told Billy that it really was very sad that he couldn't watch *Arthur*. I told him I wished I could sit and watch the show too, but I needed to wash the dishes. I told him that every boy in the world would cry if not allowed to watch *Arthur*. And every girl would cry, too.

I took my little boy in my arms, and at some point I realized that I was not performing anymore. I really was sad for him, for having to set rules which did not allow me to grant his wish.

I comforted Billy a little while, until I felt him soften in my arms. He buried his nose into my chest. I could feel the Dragon of Negativity shrinking, releasing its power over Billy's attention.

I needed a little more time before I would be able to grab Billy's attention and direct it onto something else, away from *Arthur*. So I hugged him some more and told him that he is a sweet, sweet boy. Then I asked if there might be any way to bring some happiness into his life. If I read him a book, would that make him happy? Or maybe if I would cook his favorite meal for dinner? Or if tomorrow, Friday, I let him rent a movie from Blockbuster?

I know what my boy likes, so usually I don't need to come up with more than three ideas to have him follow the pursuit of happiness. Whether it's macaroni and cheese or a dinosaur movie, he will reach out for a quick chance to get out of a tantrum.

With Billy it usually takes us about ten to fifteen minutes to complete the whole process and to settle on the next activity, which might be playing outside, or reading books, or doing his homework.

Two years ago I had to go through OMAFED several times in an afternoon. Billy was allowed to watch two agreed-upon television shows after school. So we needed one OMAFED session to get through turning the television off, a second OMAFED session to get him to do his homework, and a third if we didn't have his favorite dish for dinner.

This may seem like a lot of performing. Sometimes it was. Yet OMAFED changed our life. The change was as striking as in a "before-and-after" television commercial.

An OMAFED session can even be amusing. Just recently Billy came to my room in a state of great distress, all tears and sobbing. He felt he'd been mistreated by his sister, and he couldn't endure it. So I told him that he had every right to feel that way, that when a little boy has his feelings hurt so-o-o-o m-u-uch, he certainly needs to cry. "In fact, if anybody would hurt me so much," I said, "I'd cry so loud that I could be heard all the way to the mountains in Colorado." Billy looked at me, suddenly forgetting his crying, and said, "Mom, you can't cry *that* loud!"

"Oh," I said, "I think I could. I think if I were hurt, I could cry so loud that your cousin Steven in Nebraska would hear me!"

Then we had a conversation about how far someone could be heard crying. As Billy contradicted me, he laughed and told me I was just being silly. Then, at some point, he heard Francesca's voice, and he realized that I had tricked him out of his little drama. Poor thing, he looked at me with grand indignation, and with a heart-breaking scream, – "Daddy!" – he ran from the room. He searched for his father, hoping to recover his lost misery and find compassion. But it was too late. He'd lost the spark.

I won't try to tell you, though, that performing OMAFED is easy. It isn't. It certainly gets easier with practice, but it's always an effort – a conscious and concentrated effort.

30

A Tantrum is not Wrongdoing

Using OMAFED, I've been able to head off practically all of Billy's tantrums.

The key is simple: it's keeping the right state of mind – your own mind, not the child's. This is not easy to do, because a full-blown tantrum is like a force of nature. It affects everyone who comes in contact with it.

This morning Billy got upset that Francesca finished brushing her teeth before he did. I told him that I would try to keep Francesca from doing such a terrible thing in the future. I dramatized the situation, and, following OMAFED, told him that if Francesca would brush her teeth before *I* did, I'd probably cry for a whole long day. I gave Billy a dramatic hug; his tantrum melted in this little drama.

After about five minutes, I heard him crying in the children's bathroom again. The reason? Francesca had put their towels next to the tub, and Billy was upset that she put his towel to the right of tub and hers to the left. "Mom, ever since I was a baby my towel was *here!*" he cried, pointing to the left side of the tub. I offered him my apologies for this disastrous event. I told him that I agreed that it was a grave mistake to put his towel on the right and not on the left, and that I was about to correct it and move the towels. He stopped crying at once. He pouted though, saying, "Mom, you shouldn't joke about it."

"Oh, I'm very serious," I said, giving him a kiss.

That is the depth of Billy's emotional distress these days. It's a piece of cake.

Before OMAFED, Billy's tantrums punished all of us.

We coped.

But I kept searching for ways to redirect the energy of Billy's tantrums. From Zen and meditation, to hypnosis and energy therapy, I've tried it all. Many of these things have been of real help. But the things that helped most were those that took in both Billy and me, when I no longer separated myself from his tantrums, when I learned to suffer with him, to feel his frustration as if it was mine.

I had to learn first to let go of my judgments and not to think of a tantrum as wrongdoing. *A tantrum is not wrongdoing.* It really *is* like a force of nature. And the key to controlling it is to be aware that this is so.

I learned to think of tantrums the way a Nebraskan thinks about tornadoes.

In the little lakeside settlement where we lived in Nebraska, once in while every summer a siren would go off – the tornado warning. Do you lose your temper with a tornado? You could, but what's the point? The only thing that makes sense is to prepare – to do what my then-lawyer husband would call "exercise due diligence." Put the car in the garage, close the shutters, get the chickens into the barn. Make sure there are batteries in the flashlight, and get into the storm cellar. You do whatever you can to defend against the tornado.

So, when I started to learn to control Billy's tantrums, I'd think of a tornado. "Here it comes, beware," I'd say to myself. "It's not good, it's not bad. It's just nature at one of its extremes. Be gentle, be firm, and take over." The steps of OMAFED became my analogy to hiding the chickens, closing the shutters and driving the car out of harm's way.

When we escaped the tornado, we escaped together. Billy was aware that I was helping him out. Sometimes when it was over he'd come to me and say, "Thanks, Mom." I knew he was thanking me for managing to get us out of a tornado. His gratefulness amazed and touched me.

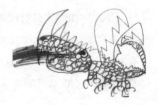

31

OMAFED and the Rest of the World

OMAFED isn't limited to autistic children. It works on anybody. It worked on me when I had PMS. It works on my daughter when she has a hard time coping with life. And guess what? It works on my husband too.

I tell my husband that it's very sad when someone has so little appreciation for a hand-made carpet that they eat crackers on it, or that they put a glass without a coaster on an oil-finished table.

I tell my daughter that it's truly unfair that she – only a child – has sorrows too great even for an adult. Poor, poor baby.

I don't know how long it will be before OMAFED comes automatically to me in response to any emotional distress that I witness. I'm certainly not there yet. But at least I'm aware now of the times when I don't follow OMAFED. I try to correct myself. Sometimes I succeed to do it right away; other times I have to wait for another chance, when I can be more collected, so that I don't start reacting to a person in emotional distress – a husband, for example – by telling him that it's ridiculous to expect children to use a coaster on an oil-finished table (and by this push him deeper into his sadness), or by telling her – a girl child – that when *I* was her age, *I* had to raise chickens and geese, *and* tend the garden, in addition to my homework (and by that make her even sadder because I don't understand her).

Oh, well.

One more thing about OMAFED. Is it hypocrisy?

What if your child is in distress because, in stubborn opposition to you, he refuses to wash his hands? If you tell him that he's right (even though he's wrong, of course), are you being hypocritical? I say you should tell him that he's right to be distressed, and that this is not hypocrisy. Although he is wrong not to wash his hands, he is right to be distressed. There's no point in telling him that he is wrong not to wash his hands until you have broken the power of the Dragon of Negativity.

When I speak to a child whose attention is arrested by the Dragon of Negativity, I actually speak to the Dragon. The Dragon is my enemy, and, to me, lying to him is not hypocrisy; it's just a part of the fight. It is a trick designed to disable a potentially devastating foe.

Yes, I'd tell the child that he is right to feel sad. I'd tell him that he has all the right in the world to feel that way. That life can be hard and painful. That his tears are precious, and beautiful as pearls. That it's OK. It's OK.

And indeed, no law says that we may not feel upset for one thing or another. So I let the Dragon know about it. I say there is no law against feeling bad. And this makes the Dragon shrink.

But I also would bring up the issue of hand-washing again, later, when the child is not in distress. I'd tell him some beautiful story about heroes who wash their hands. I'd describe to the child exactly how heroes wash their hands and that they have the courage to use both hard and liquid soap.

And this time my reasonable and sensible treatment of the subject of washing hands will not be rejected. The child will listen to my stories, and he will remember some of them. Eventually they may help him begin actually to like washing his hands, for he yearns for a chance to be a hero.

32

Happiness Training

OMAFED is a technique that I use to calm Billy during times of stress. But there are other things we can do to help reduce the stress reactions of an autistic child. One of the most important is to train him to be happy.

Yes, you can train people to be happy. Autistic children too.

Let's remind ourselves that it is common for an autistic child:

- to be negative
- to disagree
- to be withdrawn
- to be unhappy.

One way to help the child is to train his young brain how to be happy. To be happy, he needs to experience happiness. But he can't do it by himself. We need to fill the chambers of his brain with happy experiences. *Important!* These should be happy experiences that can be easily repeated or duplicated. *A lot of small happy experiences add up to much more than one big one.* One big one may even be worse than none at all.

I remember being badgered to take Billy to Disneyland. Friends were telling me that he would love it, and that, because he is autistic, I wouldn't even have to wait in lines! I didn't doubt that Billy would love it. But I knew that waiting in lines was not the problem with Disneyland. The problem with Disneyland was that the experience couldn't easily be replicated. Disneyland would give Billy such a big shot of happiness that very little in our day-to-day life would match it. Taking him to Disneyland would mean creating innumerable future temper tantrums in a child denied the chance to go to Disneyland again *today*. So I chose not to take him there. Instead, I took the path of making him happy with things he could have at any time.

I took the path of teaching him to love the beach and the forest. To love books and movies. One of our favorite routines became the visit to Monday-night story time at a bookstore a few blocks from our house. Weekend trips to rent a video have been among the high points of our life, as have trips to the bagel shop to buy fresh cinnamon-raisin bagels (Billy likes to pay for his bagel by himself), an occasional visit to a real movie theater, and popcorn at home on Friday night.

I keep the sources of joy as simple as possible.

In many homes, morning is the time when people put each other's patience to the test. Big and little people emerge from under their blankets unready for what this world has to offer. Where is the lightness of being, where are the smiles, where the joyful greeting of other family members?

It has taken months and months of training to have my children be marginally happy to see me at 7 a.m. Most of the time these days, when I approach them with, "It's time to get up, honey!" they, still sleepy, just push out their noses for a kiss. It's so sweet that I feel the angels hover above our heads.

But there are still mornings when my cohabitants are grumpy. On such mornings, I have to be very alert; for on these mornings, the path of our autistic boy seems to lead through a mine field. There could be a quick shift from grumpiness to a temper tantrum.

On such mornings, I remind myself that the Dragon is clutching at Billy's attention. I try to score "happiness points" to snatch his attention away from the Dragon. The more I succeed in bringing his attention to the world around us, the farther he gets from the Dragon.

Scoring "happiness points" is a lot of fun. People are happy when they win. Let 'em win. People are happy when they get what they want. Make them want something that you can give them.

So I make a lot of use of the Choice-Offering Tool. Every time Billy gets to make a choice, I score a happiness point – although he doesn't know it. I score a point by offering him his choice of socks. Besides the fact that he actually puts on his socks, he feels good, because it was he who chose the socks. This makes him a winner. And he loves to win.

Every time Billy gets to win, the elasticity of his attention increases. The happier he is, the less becomes the power of the Dragon of Negativity to hold on to him.

Training the elasticity of Billy's attention became one of the major elements in combating the social shortcomings that arise from his autism. Teaching him to be aware of more than one thing at a time is a big but a very rewarding task. I've noticed that the more choices/wins Billy experiences, the more balanced he is, and this makes him less open to tantrums.

It was wonderful that something as mundane as a choice of socks helped Billy feel like a winner, but the number of material choices to be made in a morning was limited; so I started creating abstract choices. If I asked Billy, "What kind of voice do you want me to read this book in: a mean voice like a witch; a loud voice like thunder; or a sweet mama voice?" his sense of winning from declaring, "Mama's voice!" was as real as the feeling he got from choosing the pair of socks he wanted.

Eventually I came to realize that it didn't matter to Billy how abstract a choice was. I found that I could even offer him something I knew he didn't want in order to get him to agree to something he would accept but wouldn't necessarily see as a "win" in the absence of choice.

Here are some examples of scoring "abstract happiness points."

"Billy, I think we should eat under the table today, on the floor."

"No, Mom! We are people! We sit on chairs."

"No, I think if we eat on the floor it will be easier to clean up afterwards."

"Mom, you're joking."

"I'm not. Well, but you're such a tidy boy. Maybe I should change my mind and let you eat at the table."

"Yes, you should!"

"OK, I give up."

Tah-Dah! Billy wins. We score some "happiness points."

We carry on this little dialog just for the fun of it – for the happiness of it. Out of little happinesses, we can build a major training campaign to win a real Battle – such as eating at the table instead of all over the house.

"Billy, I think we shouldn't go to Blockbuster today."

"No, Mom, we should!"

"Billy, it's just that it's such a hard experience. They have so many movies!"

"It's OK, Mom, don't worry. I like that they have so many movies!"

"But it makes it so hard to choose one. You'll have a hard time choosing, and I don't want you to have hard times."

"You can help me, Mom. Then it will be easy."

"Are you sure? Well, if I help you, I think you're right, it should be OK."

Tah-Dah! I not only scored happiness points, but I get to participate in choosing the movie without even having to insist on it!

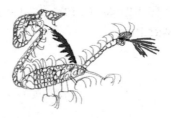

"Francesca, guess what! We're going to have garlic soup for dinner!"

"No! Not garlic soup!"

"But garlic soup is good for you. It combats germs and viruses. It makes you strong."

"But, Mom!"

"That's it! Garlic soup and a lot of it!"

"Mom, I don't like garlic soup!"

"How do you know? You've never tried it."

"I know I don't like it."

"Is it my understanding that you want me to spoil you to the point of giving you chicken noodle soup?"

"Yes, yes, please."

Tah-Dah! It works with Francesca, too. And we don't have to argue over the dinner menu.

We can craft happiness out of nothing. Out of "nothing" if we consider intangible things to be "nothing."

We can craft happiness out of imagination and creativity. You can't see them, you can't hold them, you can't buy them in a store or order them from a catalog.

All you have to do is open your heart. Open it to creating happiness out of the nothingness of imagination. It's the cheapest way. And the most rewarding.

33

Don't Say Don't

It seems to me that when we learn a language, nearly every word is supported in our memory by an image or an emotional attachment, or both. But some have much stronger support than others.

If we rank words according to their *image + emotion* power, the words "NO" and "DON'T" rank very low on the scale.

Children who misbehave are often told:

"Don't push."

"Don't touch."

"Don't scream."

"Don't cry."

"Don't splash."

"Don't scratch."

"Don't pull."

"Don't kick."

And so on.

If you think about your impressions after reading this list, you may notice that, although this is a list of "don'ts," your imagination and emotions are attached to the things which are not supposed to be done. By telling the child "don't touch," we actually reinforce his desire to touch, because, as between the words "don't" and "touch," "touch" is the word with power.

It is easier to redirect a child's attention than to stop him in his tracks by saying "don't."

For example, a child wants to play with Aunt Linda's heirloom doll. The doll is beautiful. It is also in delicate condition and likely to break. The task is to redirect the attention of the child from the doll. It is extremely hard for the child to give up the doll when all his desire is to touch it. In order to help, you need to direct his attention to something else.

Instead of "Don't touch that doll!" one needs to say something like this: "Would you do me a favor and hold this little teddy bear?" or "Can you tell how it feels to touch this stuffed frog?"

The trick is in quickly redirecting the attention. This is an important part of the training of a socially impaired child.

Our family likes to eat at the student cafeteria of a local university. The floor in the cafeteria is carpeted. Sometimes Billy lies down on the floor. It seems like a good idea to him. Telling him to stop will, most likely, cause quite a bit of stress for both of us. If I tell him to go lie down by the wall away from the tables, where he won't be stepped on, there will be no stress between us. He will probably do what I asked.

I remember the time Billy kicked a ball and hit Julia, one of his dearest friends. It hurt her. So she screamed at him, "Stop, Billy, stop!"

I took Julia aside and told her that Billy's mind, at the moment he kicked the ball, was like the ball itself: it didn't know how to think very well. Billy's mind did not know how to stop playing, just as the ball did not know how to stop moving toward her. I said to her, "If you just stand in front of the ball, Julia, it will hit you and it will hurt. But if you can push it onto a different path, it will pass by you without hurting you.

"It's the same with Billy's mind. Instead of telling him to stop, tell him something else he can do."

Since then, whenever Billy is bothering Julia one way or another, I hear her voice from the yard: "Billy, please give me that stick from the ground," or "Billy, can you come with me to the swing?" She is a smart girl, Julia.

There are many ways to redirect attention. I think the choice should be highly individualized, especially with autistic children, because they differ so much in what they like and what they are capable of doing. But redirecting attention is always much gentler than "no" and "don't." It is certainly a more respectful way of approaching a human being, and children need to be taught how it feels to be respected. Autistic children need to be taught to feel respected, too.

Among the different training tasks which I've tried with Billy, avoiding the use of negative words has been the hardest. I often hear myself saying, "Don't spill that juice!" or "Don't bother your sister!" But more and more I react in a gentler way. I try to say, "Please be careful with that cup," and "Could you please be sweet to your sister?"

The truth is, I don't like to hear negative statements myself. "Don't be nervous!" makes me nervous. "Don't be upset!" makes me even more upset. Interestingly enough, I don't like "Relax!" either. It doesn't relax me. None of these is helpful or respectful.

I'd prefer "Would you like a hug?" or "Let's go and buy some flowers." I'd prefer just being pulled away from my bothersome thoughts. Away into different dimensions. Into beauty. Into love. Into nothingness.

34

"We Use Words and Poems and Songs"

Girls play quietly; boys make noise.

I've witnessed more than a few war reenactments among boys. It's amazing how well they can understand one another by just replicating the sounds of flying bullets, roaring tanks or helicopters. It is common for autistic children – girls as well as boys – to make repetitive noises much of the time, as if they are replaying a war movie over and over and over.

We became somewhat used to Billy's noises. They helped us locate him. But, needless to say, we'd rather have lived without them.

For a long time I tried to stop Billy from making these noises. Then one day I asked him why he was always making them, and he told me, "Mom, when I don't make them, I can't hear myself! It makes me happy to make noise."

A year ago I decided to start a Battle against his noise-making. But instead of depriving him of the noise, I thought it would be good to come up with something that would help him change, yet allow him to be happy. I knew that saying "Stop making that noise!" would not help. It would just have ended up in my history of unsuccessful chaotic reminders. But I knew he does have the knowledge and the skills that are necessary to stop making noise.

I needed an approach that had more intelligence to it.

My campaign consisted of the following steps:

1. I dedicated about forty-five minutes to teaching Billy about the origin and the meaning of sound-making. I talked to him in simple terms about making sounds – that we use sounds to indicate fear or happiness, that we use words to understand each other better, and that God meant us to have some moments of silence as well.

2. I told him that people are meant to use, most of the time, words and poems and songs. That if it is hard for him to be quiet when he plays, he needs to use words and poems and songs.

3. I thought about Billy's brain. Billy is intelligent. I believed that within his brain there was a world of his own, a product of his imagination. I needed to unearth that world.

4. The next time Billy was making noise, I approached him and said, "Billy, I think there is a story in your mind."
   No reaction.
   "Billy, I think you have a story about a dinosaur in your mind."
   "No," he said, "it's about a dragon."
   "Oh. It must be about a pink dragon."
   "No, Mom! A green dragon!"
   "He must be asleep, that green dragon."
   "No, Mom. He is fighting. Fire comes from his mouth! Psh-sh-sh!" (Imitation of fire.)
   "It looks like you have a nice story about a dragon. Remember, we agreed that, when you can't be quiet, you should be using words and poems and songs. Which would you like to use?"
   "Songs. I'll sing, Mom." And he began singing a song about the fighting, fire-breathing dragon.

Billy still makes noises. But these days he will often tell and sing the story of the moment. And if the noise becomes unintelligible, it's enough for one of us to say, "Billy, we use…?" for him to reply instantly, "Yes, yes, I know. Words and poems and songs. Lah-lah-lah-lah-lah."

Since I initiated the campaign, Francesca and my husband have participated faithfully in it. They don't tell Billy to stop making noise. They ask him to use words and poems and songs. It's been a wonderful campaign. It has opened Billy to us. By helping him talk about the content of his mind, we make him feel good, even though that means he has to use words. Often Billy settles for songs, and then we hear him going about our yard singing, with a tragic operatic touch to his voice, about enemies burning to death in the fire of a mighty dragon.

More than a year after we started the campaign, we have a child who is a good storyteller. He loves telling his stories so much so that among my husband, Francesca and I, we don't have enough time to listen to them. For Billy, a good listener is a good friend. This summer my sister visited me. She doesn't know a word of English, but she is kind and patient, and so she became a dear friend to Billy. He'd come to her bed early in the morning and start telling her his dragon stories, with evil powers and courageous knights, with fierce battles and, always, happy endings. My sister listened, just watching him lovingly, shaking her head at times, making sounds that were supposed to mean agreement or wonder. Both of them were wonderfully happy!

35

The Value of Friendship

The state of our souls depends on other people. We learn how to connect socially from an early age. At three years of age, many children have favorite playmates. There are children who claim to (and do) have dear friends long before they learn how to speak well.

Billy did not have his own friends when he was three. He didn't have them when he was four or five. But by the time he was six, we started to learn how to help him in finding friendships and maintaining them.

I'll try to keep my own emotions out of my account of Billy's search for friends. I've shed my share of tears at seeing the beauty of his heart and his willingness to open it to anyone who would accept him – at seeing how he longed for a friend, how much he needed to share his devotion.

In order to make sense of my quest to find friends for Billy, I need to share with you my understanding of friendship.

Two people are friends if:

- They witness the unfolding of each other's lives.

- They mirror each other's participation in life.

- They provide support and help for each other as needed.

- They participate in an unwritten nondisclosure pact.
- They share their thoughts, their dreams and their hopes.

Under this definition of friendship, although I have many acquaintances, I have very few friends. This understanding of friendship is very Russian. If a Russian calls someone a "friend," he's not referring to someone he just drinks vodka with.

I consider friendship, in its Russian meaning, an important part of a person's social health. Finding friends and maintaining them takes time and dedication.

"Having a social life" does not mean "having friends." To me, "having a social life" is important but does not substitute for "having friends."

If "a social life" is defined as knowing many people, Billy has had one since he was four. There were more than ten children in his preschool class, there was the teacher and her assistants, and there were the specialists. But Billy did not have friends. He did not have someone to be there consistently to witness and share his life, to dream with him.

Children ordinarily develop an early need for friends. Whenever my daughter Francesca has moved to a new school, it has taken her only two or three weeks to become a part of a little circle of girls who report to each other every morning what happened to them last night. They have their secrets.

Typical children do not need to be trained to make friends. Most of them manage it on their own. They manage to find pieces of time, before class or at breaks, to connect and to feed each other with the attention and intimacy which friendship requires.

But step into a special-education class. Many children do not speak well. They do not know how to approach each other. Each of them is on his or her own, usually being shepherded by an aide in the classroom.

The class starts, the children say the pledge of allegiance, then they proceed with the curriculum.

Who is who? Does another child in the room have a family, siblings, a pet? Does another child like television or computer games? In my experience with special-education classes, the children may go through the whole year without knowing this type of information about one another. There's nothing in the curriculum that teaches how to make friends.

I remember taking Billy to school and begging the teacher to ask Billy about last night, because it was his sister's birthday party and he was excited about it and he'd love to share. And while "show and tell" times were a regular thing in Francesca's classes all the way until her fifth grade, such times have been a rarity in Billy's special-ed classes. He knew little about his teachers, about what they loved, about their families.

The children in special-ed classes spend their time in a vacuum of connections. The bus drivers change, the teachers change, the children change. Faces come and go without leaving much trace. Would it be surprising if somewhere deep, subconsciously, a child may form a fear of his own fading nature, of his unimportance, of a lack of purpose in his life?

I longed for people with whom Billy could bond. I realized that it couldn't really happen with other children in special-ed classes. They were all handicapped socially, as was he. Making a friend is hard enough for any of us. When there are socialization problems on one side, it's twice as hard. When the problems are on both sides, it's four times as hard. But Billy couldn't bond with typical boys of his age either. He was too odd for them, and they did not have patience for him.

I concluded that first Billy needed to learn to be a friend from someone who knew how to do it, who could be magnanimous about his oddities. Billy's first friend was the lady whom he calls Baba Katya, which is a Russian version of "Grandma Kathy."

Baba Katya was assigned to Billy as his aide in a special-ed class when he was five. And, indeed, although she is no longer his aide, she continues to witness his progress in life, and he witnesses her adding new laugh-lines around her eyes. They share stories. They spend wonderful times together. They have a code of conspiracy. I know that, because sometimes they stop talking when I walk into the room.

Kathy is, I suppose, a half-century older than Billy. And yet they both manage to dismiss the difference in age in favor of love and respect for one another. Billy says, "Baba Katya is my best friend in the whole wild world. She never gets mad." Kathy, I know, thinks a whole wild world of Billy.

When Billy was six I was encouraged to enroll him in an afternoon "socialization" program. The idea of the program was that several autistic children and several typical children would spend two hours a week together doing social activities – playing, having pretend tea parties, doing pretend shopping. I know that the people who organized the program had good intentions. But I had to refuse.

I refused because I believed that the program, well-intended at it was, would never lead to real bonding, to intimate and strong friendships. It did not provide enough time or the right environment. I did not want to drive Billy to "activities." It's much easier to fill in a calendar than a soul. Sometimes we get so carried away with the game of filling in the calendar that we forget to think about the soul. What is in it for the soul?

I was in charge of the course of Billy's life. Somewhere there was a clock. The hands of that clock started moving at Billy's birth, and they have been moving ever since. I felt

I had no right to waste his time on "activities" that meant little for his life. I was not interested in finding fun ways of "spending time." I didn't *want* to spend his time. This time was his LIFE TIME. I had to use it in a responsible way.

And so our grown-up friends became Billy's friends, as Baba Katya had. If you ask Billy, my friend Maruca is as much a friend to him as are her daughters, Julia and Penelope. My husband's friend, whom we call Mr Officer and who was, like my husband, a helicopter pilot in Vietnam, is a friend of Billy's. And so is his wife Cheryl. Theresa, Billy's preschool teacher, has been a faithful friend to Billy for more than four years.

Billy has learned much from his older friends. And now he is more than eight and finally ready to befriend boys of his own age. Or at least those who like dragons and dinosaurs.

I've had discussions with school psychologists about the need for children to socialize with their peers. I have a strong conviction that such a "need" is overstated. There's a "need" for strong, faithful, and loving friendships. If this happens with peers, wonderful. But if there are no peers who can provide such a relationship, ask the Lord just for a friend. Do not specify the age, the profession, or preferred hobbies. Just ask for a loving friend for your child. And when your prayers are answered and the friend comes, don't count the age. Count the blessing.

36

Sibling Shame

My friend Maruca told me this story.

Francesca was visiting her friends Julia and Penelope, Maruca's daughters. They were playing with their dolls and imagined a pretend-babies game. Julia and Penelope speculated about their own future babies – about how would they like those babies to look, what kind of things they'd like to do with their babies.

Francesca did not take part in this conversation; she just kept playing quietly with her doll. But then she raised her head and asked, "And what if your babies are autistic?"

Maruca said that both Julia and Penelope took a breath and looked at her in silence. It never crossed their minds that they might have an autistic child. It apparently crossed Francesca's mind. She knew how it might be, to have an autistic baby.

Francesca has a friend in her classroom, a quiet and lovely girl who, like Francesca, has a younger brother who's autistic. Let's call her Sophia. Just recently, Sophia's mother shared with me that sometimes Sophia is embarrassed by her brother, especially when her friends are around. His behavior seems very odd to a typical child. Not just odd, but disturbing. He makes repetitive jerking movements, hides his eyes, and doesn't communicate. This makes him impossible as a playmate and disrupts the play of everyone around him too. Children invariably come to Sophia and say,

"Can't you tell your brother to stop it?" And of course, she can't. She incurs the guilt of having him for a brother.

How does Francesca deal with Billy's autism?

We all have to tolerate our path through life, whatever path it may be; but I distinguish two kinds of tolerance. One is spiritual, the other emotional. Spiritual tolerance of the path is always of major importance. Emotional tolerance is less important.

Take the case of a soldier at war. He's more than likely to become distressed, tired, and upset, being at war. He would almost certainly rather be doing something else. But, whatever his emotions may be, to get up every morning and do his best at his job as a soldier, his spirit must be at peace with the path he is on – the path of war, like it or not. He must know that his place is there and that he is doing his job.

I think that being a sibling to an autistic child is, in a way, like being at war. Except it's a war which the sibling didn't choose. It's a war which was imposed upon her. She may feel like a victim.

It was when Billy was six that I first had to confront a situation in which Francesca was ashamed of him, in which she felt victimized by being Billy's sister. It happened while I was teaching both children in our summer home-school in a little park (see Chapter 41). I got the use of a spare room in a building in the park, and there I taught their classes. The children spent their breaks on the park playground. Children from a church summer camp nearby also came there to play.

Billy would be his autistic self. He didn't know how to play. His speech was not easily understood by children who didn't know him, nor were his ways. Francesca would sometimes overhear other kids call him "retard" and other names which embarrassed her. They brought her to tears.

And so we had a talk.

"Francesca, you are a good-looking and smart girl, right?"

"So?" She doesn't like to admit to praise, especially praise that she thinks has a hook hidden in it.

"What did you do to be born like that?"

"I don't know."

"Billy was born autistic. What did he do to be born that way?"

"I don't know."

"I don't either. But I do know that God had a reason for it, to make it happen that you were born the way you are and that Billy was born the way he is.

"Look at all these children on the playground. Look at those who were calling Billy names. Any one of them could have been autistic. Do you understand?"

"I think so."

"When babies are born, they deserve to be loved, right?"

"Of course!"

"All babies?"

"Of course!"

"What if the baby is autistic? Does that baby deserve to be loved?"

Francesca put her eyes down. "Yes," she said quietly.

"Does that baby deserve friends?"

"Yes."

"When do we start depriving an autistic child of friends? When is it time to call that child names and be mean to him? Is it OK to shun an autistic child when he is six?"

"I guess not."

"Francesca, Pumpkin, we are creatures of God. We don't get to choose the way we come to this earth. Some babies are born with diabetes, some are retarded, and some are born autistic. And each little person deserves to have a friend.

"It's understandable to find it hard to be a friend to a child with problems. But it is not right to feel superior to such a child. It is not right to feel free to harm and offend such a child."

"Yes, Mama."

"Look, you're the only sister Billy has. He can only rely on you to give to other kids an example of acceptance. If *you* are ashamed of Billy, then there must be something to be ashamed of, right?"

"I guess."

"But if you tell the other children that Billy was born autistic, and that is the way God made him and he deserves friends just like everybody else, then you will be Billy's defender. You could tell the children that they don't have to play with Billy, but that they should not hurt his feelings in any way.

"Billy can't defend himself. He just knows that nobody wants to play with him. How must that feel?"

"Not good."

"You bet. And I think there is a good reason God gave Billy a sister. Billy has the path of being autistic. Your path is to gain strength from helping Billy. By helping Billy, you will become strong and mighty. By letting shame creep into your soul, you will become weak. Do you understand?"

"Yeah."

"And now, let's train. It takes training to go against nasty kids. So I'll pretend to be the nasty kid and tease you about your brother. And you will tell me to bug off."

Francesca was shy at the beginning of our training. She'd put her eyes down and say quietly, "Don't bother my brother." It took a while to get her out of the spirit of a victim and into a spirit of a warrior, so that she could hold her head up, look into someone's eyes and say, "This is my brother. He is autistic. You may *not* hurt his feelings!"

During that summer Francesca went through a spiritual change. She accepted having an autistic brother as a part of her path in life. We spoke of God and of why things happen as they do and about our limited ability to understand why they do. We speculated about the future and about how we might be able to master it. We wondered about her future and about Billy's future. We wished for beautiful lives for both of them.

So we have created at least some spiritual tolerance to help Francesca endure her war, the war of being a sibling to an autistic child. At least for now.

As for emotional tolerance in dealing daily with the war... Sometimes there's distress, or irritation, or anger. Francesca is a good soldier. If she has her moments of emotion, that's just life. Tomorrow she will get up in the morning and start a new day. She will know in her heart that she was born at the right place, at the right time, and in the right family. And that's Dad, and Mom, and she, and Billy.

37

Books, Books, Books

Billy's autism is a long-term project. There is a clear strategy for the project – to get him fully included in life, to make him a useful, self-supporting citizen. But when working on something so big, it helps to have smaller tactical goals as well. Achieving a tactical goal helps to keep our spirits up.

One of my biggest tactical goals became teaching Billy to love to read on his own. I set this goal when he was five. It has taken us three years to achieve it.

In the beginning, he used his autistic power to insist on watching television instead of reading by himself. He didn't mind being read to, but he wouldn't make his own effort. He was ready to watch television for hours on end – or be read to, if anyone would do it – until he fell asleep. My husband and I didn't have time to do nothing but read to Billy, so getting Billy to read was a major goal. And it took a major effort.

I started that effort in the car.

Why teach a child to read in a car? Because there was no television in the car. I was driving the children to and from school every day then, about twenty minutes each way. I put a laundry basket of books between Francesca and Billy on the back seat, and I started changing its contents every ten days or so. Children love new things, and that goes for books too. Eventually, every time the children saw new books in the basket, they'd burst out in happiness.

They stopped having fights in the car – although once in a while they'd have an argument when they wanted the same book. I loved the book arguments. I loved the fact that they wanted a book so much that were willing to spend their energy on defending the right to have it. With a laundry basket full of books, such arguments were easily reduced to compromises.

My major source of books has been thrift shops. I became a frequent shopper at the thrift stores in our town. I learned which ones had the largest variety of children's books, and I bought books by the basket. At 25 to 50 cents a book, that isn't a big expense. I know I've bought myself a lot of peace for the money.

The money doesn't get you new books; but does it matter? We have books that are four or five times older than my children. Billy, when he happens to pick a really old book, runs to me: "Mom, look, this book is old and yellow. You love books like this!" Yes, I do.

Only during the last year, since I started to home-school him, has Billy really learned how to read. By the summer after his first year of home school, reading had become his number three favorite occupation. That's after watching television and playing dragon.

Interestingly, when Billy reads, he does not make the noises that his autistic brain drives him to create in abundance at all other times. So now we have chunks of time when the house is oddly quiet. Everybody's reading.

These days Billy reads the comics from our daily paper. He reads the instructions that come with a new toy. He reads the billboards and the street signs. He makes me aware of the gift of reading. Such a magnificent gift.

Billy has learned many things from reading, especially about birds and animals. He comes to share with me details about the lives of skunks or turtles, and I listen because they are news to me. There were no skunks or turtles where I grew up in the USSR. So Billy forgives my ignorance, because he knows I'm Russian. And, careful not to hurt my pride, Billy is quick to point out, "Mom, you're still smart. You're smart in Russian."

As for myself, I feel smart for making so much space for books in my children's lives. Francesca would have become an ardent reader with or without my help. Billy needed all the help he could get in his journey into the book world.

Books are my silent assistants and helpers. Day and night, they wait patiently on the shelves. They don't ask for anything. Always ready to take us traveling in space and in time, they are faithful knights in a noble service.

38

Menu, Please

One morning in August, 2000. Billy is almost seven.

For breakfast Billy eats "toasters" – peanut-butter-and-jelly sandwiches on toasted bread.

The procedure for making toasters is a matter of ritual. While the bread (no ends) is toasting, we lay out the tools and Billy specifies how many pieces he wants the toaster cut into. This morning it is four pieces. Some mornings (the only variance in the routine), he specifies "a lot a lot of pieces," which are to be stuck with cocktail forks, one fork per piece. This morning it is four pieces. "One knife for peanut butter, one knife for jelly. Cut in two pieces, cut in four pieces." That is, the bread is to be cut first in halves and then the halves into two pieces each. "This knife (the peanut butter one) on the left side; this knife (the jelly one) on the right side." He lays them on the two sides of the plastic cutting mat, which must be placed in front of the west window on the kitchen counter. The toasters must be cut on the plastic mat and then put on the plate, as Mom taught him, not cut on the plate as Dad likes to do (one less thing to clean).

But now there is a problem. There is No Peanut Butter.

Well, there is peanut butter; but there isn't Peanut Butter. For as long as Billy remembers, we have been making toasters from Skippy peanut butter. This morning there is no Skippy peanut butter on the cabinet shelf where the peanut butter belongs. There is Henry's Organic Peanut Butter, with green growing things on the picture on the jar; but there is no point in trying to pass this off on Billy as peanut butter. Dad goes to the pantry. There is no Skippy peanut butter in the pantry. The provisioner, whose name shall not be mentioned but rhymes with Mom, has not restocked the pantry with Skippy peanut butter. She has bought Jif peanut butter.

Things look bad.

Dad comes back from the pantry. He is holding a jar of Jif. Billy looks at the jar. He says, "That's not peanut butter."

"Look," Dad says. "It says, 'peanut butter.'"

Billy looks. "I'll have just jelly," he says.

Dad is happy. Instead of a major Battle, the enemy has surrendered his position without a shot.

Billy puts one knife back in the drawer. Dad takes the bread from the toaster and the jelly from the refrigerator and jellies the toast and cuts the toaster – "cut two pieces, cut four pieces." He puts the pieces on the plate and puts the plate at Billy's place at the table, and Billy sits down to eat.

Mom comes into the kitchen.

"There's no peanut butter," Dad says. "So I gave him just jelly. And he took it!" Dad sounds happy.

"There *is* peanut butter," Mom says.

Dad says, "There's no peanut butter."

Mom goes to the pantry. "Look," she calls, "there's plenty of peanut butter. Right here."

"There's no peanut butter," Dad says, feeling smart. He goes to look. She shows him. Dad says, "That's not peanut butter."

Mom shows him the label. "It says 'peanut butter' right here."

"It's not peanut butter," Dad says. "It doesn't say 'Skippy.' It says 'Jif.'"

Dad has made a mistake – there is Superiority in his voice.

Mom marches to the table with the jar of Jif not-peanut-butter. She shows it to Billy. "Look, Billy," she says in her friendliest, happiest voice, the voice of someone announcing the most wonderful discovery. "This is peanut butter!"

Billy looks with suspicion.

She points out the letters for him, one at a time. "P-E-A-N-U-T B-U-T-T-E-R." Dad thinks this is unfair, as she is pointing out only the small letters, and not the big ones that say "Jif," but Dad is a wise man and holds his peace.

Mom unscrews the lid and removes the foil cover. She sniffs. "Mm!" She holds the jar out to Billy. "Here, taste it. Put your finger in!"

Dad (although he wisely says nothing) thinks this is an unfair temptation: Billy is not allowed to put his fingers into jars.

Billy puts his finger in the jar. He gets a dab of peanut butter on his finger. He looks at the dab.

"Taste it!" Mom says in that wonderfully happy voice.

Billy tastes it.

"I hate it," says Billy.

That's the way Billy's diet went during his early years. He refused to eat new foods – even new brands of peanut butter. For a long time I was sure that he was doomed to a life of hot dogs, pizza, macaroni and cheese, french fries and ice cream. But during the past year, he has softened. His diet now includes foods which a year ago I couldn't dream he would ever eat. Billy eats corn, cauliflower, broccoli, bread and butter, mashed potatoes, chips and salsa (medium-hot), egg sandwiches, cookies *and milk*. He is willing to try new things. I am in the process of training him to substitute for his regular reaction ("YUK!!!") the expression, "This food is not quite to my taste. I'm not ready for it yet."

How did we get from his former rigidity to this lovely present?

It all started when I began home-schooling Billy. With only the two of us at home, I'd allow him to watch his favorite television show of the moment – *Between the Lions* – as he ate his lunch. Very soon I noticed that Billy was so involved with the show that he was less picky about the way his food was served. Where usually he'd fuss if I cut a sandwich in too many pieces or not enough, with the television on he'd skip the fuss and just go on and eat it. Where usually he was very particular about the size and shape of his macaroni (it had to be the round little ones), with the show in progress he'd eat even bow-shaped macaroni.

After a while I developed a plan to trick him into eating new foods.

Billy likes apples, but he had always eaten them whole only, held in the hand. He had one every day with lunch. One day I peeled an apple, cut it in little pieces and served it to him on a plate, with a fork.

"Here's your fruit, Billy."

He ate it and was happy. He ate it with the fork! He began to eat it that way daily. Then, one day, I peeled a peach and cut it in little pieces and served it on a plate, with a fork, as he was watching *Between the Lions*.

"Here's your fruit, Billy."

It looked pretty much like his regular fruit, and because he was watching his show, he didn't pay much attention anyway. Before he knew it, Billy was eating peaches. He came to like them. After about a month I served him a pear.

I certainly try to be careful with my experiments. I would not offer something far out of his range, like mango or passion fruit.

Another success was melted butter. I got Billy to try broccoli with melted butter. At first he was intrigued by the mechanics of having a little bowl with hot melted butter, of putting some salt on top of it, of dipping a piece of broccoli in it. He tried it for the sheer experience, and he liked the buttery, crunchy feeling of the broccoli. Also, the words "with melted butter and salt" became the locomotive for introducing other foods. Now he will eat cauliflower dipped in melted butter and salt, mashed potatoes with melted butter and salt, fresh-baked bread with melted butter and salt.

I use the word "locomotive" because in the old days, when I lived in the USSR, any poet who wanted his book to pass the censors knew he had better have a "locomotive poem." The "locomotive poem" was the song of praise to the Communist Party. It need not have anything to do with the rest of the book or to show any poetic talent. Its job was to drag the rest of the book to publication.

And so "with melted butter and salt" is our locomotive. It drags new foods along. Maybe one of these days Billy will try spinach with melted butter and salt. Or is that taking it a bit too far?

We still work on table manners, though.

One evening I happened to drop off something at Maruca's house right at dinner time and was invited to join her family at the dinner table. Maruca served the meal, with her husband and children helping. Then she sat down and DID NOT GET UP until dinner was finished. I was quite taken by this, because, at our house, I'd have to jump from my chair many times during dinner.

Dining with Billy would make anyone jump. Things get spilled, the tablecloth gets pulled, the chairs get rocked (whether or not they are rocking chairs). The butter or the ketchup gets spread around; the salt is dumped in piles. And so on.

Billy also eats fast and is done before everyone else. I often serve him his dessert before anyone else is done with the main course. He can't wait. I don't mean, "He doesn't want to wait." I mean, "He is not capable of waiting." I don't see a point in making him sit and wait for ten minutes until everybody else is ready for dessert. Those ten minutes would become an endless challenge. He'd be up and down, running to look at the clock every thirty seconds. By the time dessert would come, we'd all be tired of each other.

So Billy goes through his meal as efficiently as he fancies. When he's done, he says the magic words and goes about his business. Francesca, though, likes to sit with us. She likes to talk and to listen to us talk. And she has her dessert together with everybody else.

I've told you how bad Billy's restaurant manners were in the beginning. They didn't improve for several years. When Billy was six, some members of our family from Nebraska visited us in San Diego. We wanted to take them to a nice place for dinner. We went to a restaurant right on the water at San Diego Bay. We took Billy with us, hoping that the passing boats would distract him enough that we could survive a dining-out experience. No such luck. Billy was not interested in the passing boats. Instead, he was interested in the salt shakers. He became determined to collect the salt shakers from all the nearby tables. We couldn't change his mind. We ended up dragging him out of the place. We went to the car. We felt bad, because we had placed our orders already, and we had built up in our guests the expectation that they'd have a really good meal. I asked my husband to go back and make sure that they did. I stayed outside and entertained Billy until they were done.

Things hadn't gone quite as we intended; but Billy was happy eating his french fries outside, and I was happy that our guests could have a good time without him.

Only when Billy was seven did he become restaurant-broken. In that year, we went to a restaurant with the children, and when the meal came, we realized that Billy had actually sat in his place and kept busy right up to that moment, drawing on his placemat (a kid's placemat the restaurant provided, along with crayons).

Now we can go with Billy to practically any restaurant, as long as we make sure that the menu has something acceptable to him. We need to be well prepared to entertain him for the full time in the restaurant. We need to have paper and markers for him to draw and write, and we know we'll have to dedicate our time to engaging him in games – writing rhyming words or doing some fun math. Of course, this will not be relaxing time spent together. It will be dining out while keeping Billy from bothering anyone (or everyone) else in the place.

Even so, his average tolerance span for such an endeavor is about thirty minutes. After that he tells us, "Let's go home, I'm tired."

Our favorite place to dine is in Alpine, a half-hour east of San Diego. It's a restaurant with a number of outdoor tables. There's a little pond, lovely trees and lots of grass. We place the order, and then the children play around the pond and in the grass. They come back to the table when the order comes.

Billy also loves going to Denny's. They have good french fries, and they loan every child a little bucket of plastic construction toys. One day Billy was so inspired by "the guy whose name is Denny and who set up such a good restaurant" that he decided that, when he grows up, he will set up his own restaurant. He'll name it Billy's, and the place will serve french fries, macaroni and cheese, hot dogs, apples, apple juice and chocolate ice cream.

Well-Meaning People

People who have no experience with autistic children, seeing one in action, often think that this child is just extremely ill behaved. And in fact the child *is* extremely ill behaved, if the normal standards of child behavior are applied. It's certainly true that many autistic children are extreme versions of an unruly child. Their parents, in time, develop a semi-immunity to their behavior. After all, parents have the benefit of parental instincts, such as protectiveness and love.

Strangers often don't see a child as the parents do. And strangers who don't know autism not only won't understand why the child is acting that way, they probably won't understand, when the parent acts to calm the child or protect him from himself, why the parent is acting that way either.

Sometimes they think it is their duty to interfere.

It is unfortunate, but true, that every parent of an autistic child needs to be prepared to defend herself, and to defend her child, against well-meaning people.

Sometimes the well-meaning person is the one who is going to call the police. For example:

For his first six years or more, we could never predict what might happen when we were out with Billy. Once while we were out shopping, Billy had to go to the bathroom. I couldn't think of a public bathroom nearby, so I stopped at a fast-food place. We went in. Billy took along the cotton ball which he had been holding in his hand all morning for comfort. After a while, I heard him crying in the men's room. It was a one-person restroom, so I opened the door to see what was the problem. Billy was in tears. He had lost his cotton ball. I didn't have another cotton ball at hand. I tried to persuade him to come out, to no avail. Finally he spotted his cotton ball. I saw it, too, but it was in a place so unsanitary that I couldn't possibly let him have it. So I didn't have any choice but to grab him and carry him out of the place. He was screaming and trying to escape. When we got to the car, he refused to sit in it, kicking and hitting everything around him with his feet and his hands. I was sweating, my nerves and muscles all strained from trying to deal with the situation, hoping to break the intensity of his tantrum. Just then a young woman, dressed as if for a night club, came up to me and told me to stop torturing the poor boy. I had used up so much of my tolerance on Billy that I didn't have any left for her. "Go away!" I snapped, keeping my eyes on Billy to make sure that he didn't hurt himself.

"I'll call the police!" said the young woman. She shook her cell phone in her hand.

"Go ahead," I said.

The woman started dialing. I knew this was no joke. I knew I couldn't deal with the police at that moment. I would have felt so humiliated at having to explain that I have an autistic son and that this is a temper tantrum, that my autistic child is temporarily out of balance.

I locked the doors of the car and drove away with Billy kicking and hitting the seats and the windows of the car. I drove several blocks, to a little park I knew, and stopped the car there. There was no one around. And there I went through my "buying time" technique. (At that time I didn't know yet how to do OMAFED, which is more efficient.)

I told Billy that I loved him very much. That I would get him many, many cotton balls. And again, that I loved him. That I couldn't drive until he calmed down. If we didn't drive, we would not get home. If we don't get home, we can't watch television.

Slowly, he subsided – from rage, to tears, to sobbing, and finally to a sigh of relief. We hugged, and we were ready to drive home.

Francesca was with us. All the time she just sat quietly in the car and tried to follow my directions to her: "Hold on, Pumpkin, you know Billy, he'll be OK soon. Hold on, Pumpkin." And she did.

Sometimes the well-meaning person is not someone who threatens to call the police: sometimes it *is* the police.

Once when Billy was two, I had the children in the car when I arrived at a fabric shop where I intended to buy one thing – some fabric for a blanket, I think. The children were asleep in their car seats. They were warm and cozy, and as I entered the parking lot by the store and looked at their dreaming faces, I knew that if I woke them up Billy would have a major tantrum. Tantrums are hard not only on me. They are hard on Billy himself; they are hard on Francesca. Every time I could avoid one, I gave it a shot.

So I decided not to wake them. I parked the car right in front of the glass door of the store on the "Loading Zone" line. I went into the store, and as I stood inside the door, I waved the manager over to me. I showed her my children in the car (three yards from the door) and I told her that I had to stay by the door to watch them, but maybe she could be so kind as to find the fabric I wanted. While I waited by the door, my eyes on the children, I saw a policeman approach the car and start writing on his pad. I supposed he was giving me a parking ticket. I stepped out of the store and greeted him.

He said, "Ma'am, I want you to follow me to the police station."

"Why?" I asked.

"It's child abuse to leave your children alone like this. We need to go to the station, and the officer in charge of these sorts of crime will take over your case."

I refused to go, which I think surprised him. I said, "I'm not going to the station, sir. If you're referring to the children being in the car while I was in the store, then maybe you'll have a different understanding after you talk to the manager inside. I stood by the door all the time, and I didn't lose sight of my children. I refuse to go to the station because I have done nothing wrong. And I can't be forced to go unless you have a warrant for my arrest."

My husband the lawyer said later that it usually is not a good idea to talk to a policeman that way – nor good law either, as he didn't really need a warrant to arrest me if he thought I was committing a crime. Oh, well. It worked this time. The policeman talked to the manager. I'm grateful for her willingness to talk to him and back up my words. So many people avoid talking to the police. But she did, and through that she may have saved us a humiliating courtroom ordeal.

After he talked to the manager, the policeman no longer insisted on taking us in, but he still said the officer in charge of child abuse would contact me.

Shaking from sadness, anger, and helplessness, I drove home. The children, thank God, slept sweetly through all of this. When my husband came home from work I told him the story, and it certainly killed his taste for dinner.

The officer in charge of crimes like mine did call, eventually, and he also talked with the store manager. He decided not to prosecute me.

There are no good ways to prevent public tantrums and misbehaviors. If they are going to happen, they'll happen. Nor is there any way I know of to prevent well-meaning people from trying to protect your child from you.

The only thing I know of that might be useful is to carry with you a card saying that your child is autistic and explaining, in simple terms, what autism is and what an autistic tantrum is.

Such cards were once offered by the Autism Society of America. The national organization no longer has them, but some of its local chapters still may. I wish I'd had a card when Billy had his tantrum over his lost cotton ball. (When the policeman wanted to take me in, I didn't even know Billy was autistic.) I think it would have helped the well-meaning woman understand what was going on. As it was, the conclusions she drew must have been based on her experience with typical children. But experience with typical children is not necessarily helpful in dealing with autistic children; and I didn't have time to educate her.

Many people, though, have heard enough about autism to be compassionate when they are told that a child is autistic. I remember a waitress at Denny's who was very impatient with Billy, who was climbing up and down the back of the booth where we were sitting. When I told her that our boy is autistic, her attitude changed immediately. Her impatience vanished, and she waited on us with special care.

Similarly, my husband was recently at the public library with Billy, looking for children's videos. Billy found one that excited him and, in his excitement, he ran to show it to his dad. The only problem was that they were in a narrow aisle between the shelves and there was an old man between them. It's hard for many autistic children – Billy among them – to keep in mind the rules of polite public behavior even when they aren't excited. They don't understand, at an emotional level, that most people don't like to be touched by someone they don't know. And when an autistic child is excited, a person in the way is just an obstacle to be moved. So Billy pushed past the old man.

The man said, to no one in particular, but in a very sarcastic tone, "Oh, kids these days! They've got no idea how to behave in public!"

Billy's father was aghast. He insisted that Billy apologize – which Billy did, but in a perfunctory way; his mind was still on his video. Billy's father also explained that Billy is autistic, and the man's attitude immediately changed. "Oh, I thought the boy was just being rude," he said.

And of course, the boy was. By the usual standards.

But Billy's father appreciated the man's compassion.

Sometimes I think this compassion is triggered by people's feeling sorry for the parents who won the ticket that said, "Autistic child for YOU!" People feel lucky that they didn't win one themselves.

But I truly don't care what triggers this compassion in people. I'm just grateful for it.

40

A Special Education

Billy's preschool year was a blessing to us because of Theresa.

His kindergarten year went by without any major events. He didn't learn much; he did not cause many problems. But our experience that year made us aware that we could not just rely on the San Diego Unified School District to provide an education for Billy. There are a lot of special-education classes in the SDUSD; but we now knew that not all of them were as good as Theresa's.

We spent the spring of Billy's kindergarten year looking at special-ed classes. With our friend Bobbi, a psychologist in the school district's special-education department, we visited schools and sat in on classes and talked to teachers. We found what we thought was the perfect class for Billy, a special-education class taught by a lovely, organized woman teacher who spoke barely above a whisper, yet kept perfect order and organization in her class. We asked that Billy be placed in her class, and we took our summer off, well pleased.

First grade
Two weeks before school was to start, we were informed that Billy would be in a completely different class in a completely different school. The teacher we admired had been assigned to a regular second-grade class.

We hurried to meet Billy's new teacher. He was a fine man who had taught autistic children in seventh and eighth grades. He seemed capable. So Billy went off to his special-ed class.

The class had a total of eight children. All of them had behavior problems; many of them had serious behavior problems. Nearly all of them had their own aides; so there were a lot of people in the classroom. Some of the aides had no training. It was not long before I started worrying.

I went to observe Billy's classroom. While observing, I made notes about what was happening there. At one point, I registered forty-eight disciplinary remarks by the teacher during one hour of teaching.

My judgment of the classroom environment was simple: if it would be hard for me to learn in such an environment (and it would), how could I expect a child with learning disabilities to do it?

As we learn, our brains store information. As we grow, we draw upon the wealth of information accumulated there. If there isn't a math file in the brain, we probably won't know how to do fractions. If there's no grammar file, we don't know grammar.

The information which gets stored in the brain could serve some use in life, or it could be trash. There are trashy television programs, but the only places that get trashed in the process of viewing these programs are the brains of the people who watch them.

When children watch commercial television programs, the commercials present a flood of trash information to their brains. They store everything they're exposed to. That's why it's so important for the parents to choose what to expose their children to. It's our job.

If I learn a new language, and the teacher as a joke teaches me to say something wrong, I have no way of knowing it. I'll just repeat what I've learned like a parrot, to the delight of those who know the joke.

For a child with learning disabilities, the process of learning math or grammar or reading is somewhat like learning a foreign language. And if the instruction comes half-and-half with disciplinary remarks, that's how it gets recorded in the brain: "We put a period at the end of a sentence take your shoes off the table." The second part of information is not necessary for the purposes of learning to complete a sentence, but it gets stored in the child's brain nevertheless. It goes into the brain even though it is trash information. The children in some special-ed classes accumulate a lot of trash.

I couldn't change the system to provide a better alternative for all the children in special education, but I felt it was my obligation to look for a better place for my son.

In November, with the school district's agreement, we moved Billy to a new school – the one we had wanted to send him to in the first place, although with a different teacher. Baba Katya was still his full-time aide. His new teacher was Ms Robinson. It was a special-ed class, but the boys in the class did not have severe problems. Billy, actually, was the problem child; but Ms Robinson came to like Billy a lot, and he liked her and was proud of her and wanted her to be proud of him. Ms Robinson believed that Billy was smart and could make good academic progress. With her help he started to read beginners' reading books. Kathy worked hard with Billy as well. And yet I felt that the distractions in the classroom made it hard for Billy to concentrate on learning.

Slowly though, he learned. He made new friends. Things were going OK, I thought. Then one day in the spring of that school year, Ms Robinson did not come to school. She never came. She had a heart attack and died in her sleep.

She was a Buddhist. I attended the service which her family and friends had for her, and I learned that they were convinced that she had reached Buddhahood. I believe it too.

They asked me if I wanted to say something. I got up and spoke about Billy and what a hard child he was, but how, whenever Ms Robinson had to report to me some misbehavior by Billy, she faulted herself. She'd tell me, "I know it's my fault. I did not give these children enough love, and that's why they misbehaved. I just need to go home and pray more so I can give more comfort to these children."

Billy, socially inept as he was, so unaware of many basic things in life, was very aware of Ms Robinson's absence from the world. He was aware of her death, and he mourned his teacher. He'd tell the waitress in a restaurant, or anyone who would listen: "My teacher died. She was black. Her name was Ms Robinson. She had a big smile." And there was so much sadness in his little face.

Ms Robinson died near the end of Billy's first-grade year. The woman who was assigned to teach her class tried hard, but she was inexperienced, and she didn't have Ms Robinson's depth of love for the boys in the class. Billy's learning slowed. In any case, he would have lost Ms Robinson at the end of that year – another school year, another classroom, another teacher, on to the next grade. We spent that spring, too, looking through the elementary schools of San Diego with Bobbi, looking for the right place for Billy.

We found what seemed the best place for him – a special-education academy for children with learning disabilities. But...

But what?

But I wasn't at peace with special education.

41

Summer School

From my childhood I associated the end of a school year with a grade report which children bring home to their parents as a testimony to their increased knowledge.

When Billy finished his first grade, he brought home a grade report. It reflected his behavioral problems, but it definitely was not a testimony to his increased knowledge. Billy knew some things. He could count to ten, he could read sentences like "Fat cat on the mat." Our daughter is only two years older, so we still remembered how much she knew when she graduated from her first grade – much, much more than Billy knew.

At the same time, Billy's knowledge, whatever he had actually acquired at that time, was somewhat mechanical. I couldn't help being reminded of a dog who had been trained to count if he gets the right treat. I wondered how far Billy was from the trained dog. I knew that the teachers in his special-education classes used treats as incentives. Often they used candy. There were many times when I tried to intervene, but eventually I realized that I couldn't change the system. And, after all, what did I have to offer instead? A treat that works so well on a dog works on a child, and for the same reasons. And it helps the trainers in their work.

I asked a psychologist about Billy's future prospects; but that was like asking a doctor about the outcome of a treatment. I got a list of options. At the top was, "He may be OK." At the bottom was,

"He may be institutionalized." I didn't like the bottom option. So I thought that the time had come to undertake a project. I needed to learn for myself whether Billy was retarded. I needed to make sure that, if the bottom option became the only one, I'd know that we had done everything possible to help him reach one of the others.

I started a summer school to see for myself what Billy could do.

I didn't think that our house would be a good place for an autistic child to start learning from his mother. There are too many distractions at home. So I started looking for another place. I found a corner in a game room at a clubhouse in a small park of the San Diego Department of Parks and Recreation.

Going to the park manager with my request to use the space, I was apprehensive. I didn't think it would be something she was used to hearing: "Ma'am, I have an autistic child. I need to summer-school him. Please help." Well, as Jesus said, ask and it shall be given. The manager said, "OK, we'll help you. Just fold the tables and the chairs after you're done. And keep out if there are any games scheduled." There were never any games scheduled. The room was always empty, ours to use.

My school supplies were in a large traveling bag which I dragged from my car to the game room every morning. We'd unfold one desk and several chairs, and we were ready to start.

Our summer school lasted for about six weeks. Every morning we had three classes, with thirty minutes of study followed by fifteen minutes of play on the park playground. The playground became Billy's incentive for learning. To me, that was a much better incentive than candy, further from pure animal training. But my final goal was to teach Billy that the pleasure of learning was an incentive in itself. It seemed a far-fetched goal that summer; but eventually we've got there. Not that the road has been easy. And it's still a rocky one.

But during that summer school I got my first glimpse into Billy's hidden intelligence. I had to plow through a lot of resistance before Billy would accept any new knowledge. Anything new was like a red scarf to a bull. I still have a clear memory of Billy bent over our school desk, wailing through tears, "I hate minus! I hate minus!"

That was the second week of our home schooling. I thought that since he already knew that two frogs plus two frogs makes four frogs, it was time to tell him that four frogs minus two frogs would make two frogs.

By the end of our summer school, Billy was fine with the concept of "minus." But he didn't learn as much during those six weeks as I did. I learned that his attention span was close to zero. Even when he looked as if he were paying attention, his mind might be wandering God knows where. I learned that Billy's body, constantly on the move, was a big distraction for him. I learned that if a typical person needed x repetitions to remember something, Billy needed $10x$, $20x$, or sometimes $100x$.

I could teach him a new notion on Monday, and on Tuesday he'd act as if he'd never heard of it. But on Wednesday there would be a spark of recognition. After teaching the same thing day after day, by Friday Billy could actually, sometimes, remember it.

During that summer I learned that reading actually came easily to Billy, but that abstract reasoning was hard on him. He didn't have a problem with one-step instructions: "This is how you say this word." He had a lot of trouble with instructions of two steps or more: "If you take six pens and add one pen, that makes seven pens."

I learned that the logic of even simple mathematics was not obvious to Billy, as we expect it to be to any one. To Billy, six frogs plus one frog might well be nine frogs, because he could imagine the two extra frogs. The logic of our world was sifted through the logic of his world, and I discovered that he had a huge world of his own. That world has different dimensions and different laws than ours. His world was much more flexible than ours. In his world he could fly and meet dragons. In his world there was no problem making nine frogs out of six plus one.

I was trying to impose the rigidity of our world on him, and he protested greatly. That six plus one is seven, and always so, and couldn't be otherwise, is a great imposition, if you think so. And Billy thought so.

But I learned in our summer school that Billy could be taught, one on one, if the teacher had 100 percent alertness, all of it directed to Billy's attention, Billy's moves, Billy's thinking, Billy's emotions. It was a hell of a job, and there was no one applying for it. So I had to take it.

After summer school, we went to Nebraska to visit our extensive family. It was show-off time for Billy and me. At every visit, I made him read for his relatives. He demonstrated his math accomplishments too, even if they were less spectacular. Billy loved the attention. That summer he learned that knowledge, if nothing else, may bring the attention of a crowd, and for him this was the highest incentive that could exist.

I received lots of praise for being a good, dedicated mom. I enjoyed the praise. But I knew better. I knew that this was just the beginning. My dedication was going to be put to the test over and over again. We'd still have to go through "I hate multiplication" and "I hate division," and other hates yet unknown, before we could again go for a visit to show off.

42

The Academy – and Home at Last

Second grade

That fall we enrolled Billy in the special-education academy that we had decided on before Billy's summer school.

The academy was well funded and well staffed, with teachers dedicated to special education. Billy's class was of twelve boys. They worked in groups of only three children and rotated among teachers throughout the day. Baba Katya was still Billy's aide. Our hopes were high.

But within a very short time I began to feel that the environment at the academy was too difficult for a child like Billy. The problems were partly educational and partly social.

Because of the rotation system, Billy was taught by a minimum of four different teachers daily. As a result, no one knew well his strong and his weak points. I tried to work with Billy at home and to coordinate my work with the work at school. I failed. I would have needed at least thirty minutes a week of conference time with his teachers, but they were not paid for that. I can't begrudge their not volunteering to work with me gratis.

On top of these educational problems, some of Billy's autistic behaviors, which had improved so greatly during our summer program, started to deteriorate again. Copy-cat that he is, he was making every noise that other children made and exhibiting every behavior that another child exhibited. And they all made noises and showed unusual behaviors. It was not their fault. They couldn't help it. I understood perfectly. Hadn't I lived with Billy for six years? But yet… But yet I didn't want him acquiring their problems, any more than I wanted them to acquire his.

After six weeks of weighing all the pluses and minuses, I told my husband that I was thinking about taking Billy out of the academy and home-schooling him.

My husband thought that the task of teaching an autistic child was too much for one person. Especially if that person was the parent, which meant nonstop care for an autistic child.

We asked Theresa, our kind arbiter, to come for tea. She too warned me that it would be a hard road.

They were right. It was hard.

I started our home school in October. We changed my sewing room to a classroom, and I put up on the wall a framed, embroidered sign with the name of our school: "The Aristotle School for the Bright and Gifted."

In spite of the brave sign, I had dreadful fears of failing. There were moments when I felt inept. My Reserves points were in the red for weeks on end.

But there is a God in Heaven. I had faith in God, and to God I brought all my fears, all my ineptitude. I asked for help, and help came. It came from places which I couldn't have predicted. It came from people whose help I didn't expect.

It was in February that, one day, in the midst of a class, Billy looked at me and said, "You're a good teacher now, Mom." And the angels sang "Hallelujah!"

In March the school district was able to find an aide for Billy, and he began to spend two afternoon hours four times a week in a regular classroom. The combination of home-schooling and a regular classroom proved to fit his needs. I was in control of his academics, and he did his socializing at school.

Billy's home-schooling will need a separate book. There was struggle aplenty for both Billy and me. But from being outraged at the idea of being stuck to a desk for several hours, and from hating the idea of having to learn rather than play, Billy went to being proud of learning. After a year of home-schooling, Billy was given three comprehensive tests at his regular school. The results were marvelous: he tested at or above his age level in all subjects.

We've continued the same program this year: home-schooling in the morning for academics, and regular school in the afternoon for socializing. When I asked Billy if he'd like to be in the regular school full time, his answer was, "Let me think about it. Mmmm...I don't know, Mom. Your school makes me smart." So we keep going.

Billy loves The Aristotle School. One teacher in the school. One student. Lots of love. It's amazing what love can do.

43

Epilogue: The Four Stages of Life

In the Moldavian village where I grew up, it was impossible not to be aware of the continuity of life. The village children witnessed the celebrations of couples getting married, of new babies being born. When someone in the village died, we followed the funeral procession all the way to cemetery and watched the earth swallow the coffin and listened to the wailing women. We saw the orchards bearing fruit and the fields filled with crops. We saw puppies born. We witnessed the magic of a new, warm calf just out of his momma.

We had the comfort of fitting into a social structure which carried people through life. We knew how birth approached, and death. We knew what we could expect to do when we became adults. We knew that as we grew we would be expected to take charge and carry out the jobs and the rituals of elders.

There was a continuity in life for us.

Thinking about this, I realized that it is impossible to overstate the value in my own life of this awareness of continuity.

I thought of Billy. Is there a continuity of life in his heart? How do I make him love our world? How do I make him feel a precious part of life on the Earth?

And I told him a story:

"See the stars, Billy, high in the sky. Those stars are souls, Billy. When they are ready, they come to the Earth. They talk to God and tell God that they'd like to come to the Earth as a boy, or as a girl, and they tell God which family they'd like to be a part of.

"And so, once upon a time, your soul was a star. One day your soul was ready to come to the Earth as a boy named Billy, a boy born to Daddy and me, with Francesca as a sister. Your soul asked God if it was OK, and God thought about it, and he thought that it was a good idea.

"We begot a boy, and your soul-star descended gently to house in our new baby. When you were big enough, we had to take you out of my tummy.

"And so your journey on the Earth started.

"Your journey on the Earth has four stages.

"The first stage is *Survival*, from the time you're born until you're three.

"In this stage you're just a baby. All you need to do is sleep, and eat, and be happy. Your parents are fully responsible for all your needs. They feed you, dress you, bathe you, and take care of your tears.

"Stage two is *Learning How to Survive*. This stage lasts from four to six.

"During this stage you learn how to do things for yourself. You learn how to eat properly, how to dress, how to wash yourself. You start learning how to read and write. In this stage, your parents start sharing responsibility with your teachers, in order to make sure that you learn how to survive.

"Stage three is *Learning the Rules of the Earth*. This stage goes on from age seven until you are seventeen.

"Now the responsibility is shared by your parents, your teachers, and you. During this stage you need to learn what it means to be a human being. You learn about other human beings and the ways they live. You learn how to work. You learn how to make peace. You learn how to love other people and how to let other people love you.

"Stage four is *Becoming a Wise Man*. This begins when you are eighteen, and it lasts for the rest of your life.

"And then the responsibility will be all yours. When you are eighteen, you are expected to know a lot and to start acting on your own to become a wise man. You can still have the help of your parents or of teachers, but that will have to be your choice."

Billy loved the story. He loved to be connected to the stars.

We return often to this story. For Billy, who was not born with an innate sense that anyone has authority over him, it has provided a structure within which he can accept the authority of a teacher. It has helped him see himself as a part of a bigger scheme. He knows now that God has a plan for him. He also knows that he himself has a responsibility for the way his life will unfold.

Often these days, when Billy frowns at the prospect of learning something new, I just tell him that he has to do it because it's a part of learning the rules of the Earth.

"Are you eighteen yet?" I ask.

"No," he answers, and succumbs to learning, knowing that he is, still, at the stage of Learning the Rules of the Earth.

There are still many rules of this Earth for Billy to learn. It's amazing how many of them human beings have invented. Some rules are very hard to follow. The rule of sitting still for hours in a classroom is hard, and so is the rule of not being allowed to play tag on the schoolground. I often think that it would have been easier for a child like Billy to grow up on a ranch, with plenty of space and freedom around him. And it might have been even easier for him to grow up as a Native American in times long gone, riding a horse and hunting the buffalo. It seems to me that the rules of the Earth in those times and places would have been easier for our Billy to follow.

But we are here, in the heart of San Diego, at the beginning of the third millennium. We have to do our best with what we've got. And even though we do not have a village with its old rituals to support us, or the endless freedom of the prairies, we have everything that really matters, regardless of time or place. We have the soil under our feet and the blue sky above our heads. And in the dark we have the stars burning for us. And each star is a precious soul waiting for a mother and father to welcome it to the Earth as a boy or as a girl. Mind you, some of those boys or girls may happen to be autistic.

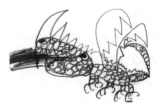

Appendix: Billy's Words at Age Four

English

Are you OK?
book
boo-boo
bubbles
cat, kitty
clean up
close it
come back
daddy
dog, doggie
don't
duck
flush
get down
give me…
good boy
goodbye
hello
hit
horse
lion
milk
mommy
night-night
no (or NO!)

oh, yuck!
oink
pig
please
quack
quiet
rabbit
sit down
soda
straw
table
thank you
very good!
what's the matter?
where
where's
you're welcome

Russian

basin (*swimming pool*)[1]

domoi (*home*, as in *let's go home*)

gdye (*where at*)

izbushka (literally *a little log hut*, but it's what we called our family room)

kartoshka (*potatoes*)

kholodno (*cold*)

knizhka (*book*)

kotyik (*little cat*)

kuda(*where to*)

kupalnik (*swimsuit*)

kurochka (*chicken*)

kushat (*eat*)

loshadka (*little horse*)

moloko, molochko (*milk*)

slomalas (*it's broken*)

soda

sok (*juice*)

spaht (*sleep*)

trewsiki (*little trousers*)

upal (*it fell* or *I fell*)

zaichik (*little rabbit*)

---

1   A number of the Russian words – *basin* (prounced ba-seen), *kupalnik*, *kholodno* – probably were in Billy's vocabulary only because our house had a swimming pool. Also, although I've mentioned that one of Billy's first words was the Russion *poyezd* (train), by age four he had completely forgotten it – trains were not a part of our life in San Diego.

Index

aggression
  during tantrums 24
  towards other children 23, 53
animal impersonations
  dragon impersonations 52, 54,
    55, 106
  on waking 103–4, 105–6
attention-span 54, 187
autism
  coming to terms with 42–4
  common manifestations 39
  diagnosis 33–6
  one boy's history 45–57
  recognition 37–40
autism cards 179
Autism Society of America 179

baths
  bedtime ritual 68
  morning ritual 73–4
  tantrums 29–30
Battles 111–13
  Battle-plan example 114–16
  in progress 120–2
  repetitive noise 152–4
  and Reserves 101, 112, 115, 118
  Sock-Battle considered 117–19
bedtime
  "buying time" 62
  ritual 67–70
biting 23, 32

books 47, 165–7
  at bedtime 68–9
brain chambers 127–9
breakfast ritual 74
brushing (whole-body) 97–8
"buying time" 61–5

California 31, 95
chaotic (serial) reminders 111, 113,
    117, 119
chewing on clothes 48, 52
ChOT (choice-offering tool) 86–93
  and "happiness points" 145
church 55–6, 75–6
climbing 22–3
Communists 67, 172
Connecticut 11, 16, 20, 95
continuity 192
cotton balls 48, 176

deviations from routine 33–6
diet *see* food and diet
Disneyland 143–4
"dont's" 149–51
Dragon of Negativity
  pre-menstrual syndrome 129–32
  shrinking with OMAFED 133–4,
    142
  using "happiness points" 144–5
dressing, using ChOT 87

early-intervention programs 16
eating *see* food and diet
emotional strength 43–4

Enlightenment check 41
eye contact 39, 45, 47, 48

Fashion Careers College, San Diego
    33–4
first grade 53–4, 181–4
fixations 39
food and diet 168–74
    breakfast choices 74
    expanding the menu 53, 56,
        170–2
    limited and rigid tastes 14, 39,
        46, 47, 168–70
    secret chocolate-eating 48–9
    table manners 172–3
    using ChOT 87
four stages of life 192–5
friendships 155–9

getting up 73–4, 103–4
"good" and "bad" children 42–3

hand-washing 142
handsomeness 39–40
happiness training 143–8
Hobbit, The (cartoon) 50
home school 55, 58, 190–1

Japanese factories 90

Kazakhstan 15, 16
kindergarten 52

"limitless terms" 127
"locomotives" 172
Lord of the Rings, The (animated film)
    50

marital relationship
    disagreements over handling
        autism 107–10
    and pre-menstrual syndrome
        125–31
massage 98–9
mathematics 54–5, 57, 187–8
memorizing dialog 50–1
Miles, Theresa 51, 58–60, 61,
    109–10, 159, 181
Moldavia 42, 66–7, 192
mornings
    happiness training 144–5
    ritual 73–4
    schedules 77–9, 103
    starting the day 103–6
    warming clothes 109–10
Moscow 96, 97

nannies 20–1
Nebraska 31, 42, 96, 139, 188
New Year's Eve celebrations 123–4
New York City 10, 16, 26, 27, 31,
    95
night-time snack 53, 69–70
nurseries 21–2

occupational therapy 16, 97–8
OMAFED (Open-Minded
   Assistance for the Emotionally
   Disturbed) 133–42
   heading off tantrums 138–40
   and the rest of the world 141–2
   shrinking the Dragon of
      Negativity 133–4, 142
   using 135–7

parenting
   Reserves 100–2
   "rights" and "wrongs" 11–12
   warrior-parents 111–13
physical sensitivities 94–9
playgrounds 10, 22–3, 47, 54,
   79–81
   behavior schedule 80–1
   sibling shame 161–4
poetic communication 83–5
police 177–8
potty and toilet training 46, 47,
   49–50, 52, 54
prayers
   child's 56, 76
   parent's 104–5
pre-menstrual syndrome (PMS)
   125–31
preschools 31–2, 51
"Princess Touch" 69
promise ritual 70–2
public tantrums 27–8, 96
   well-meaning people 175–7
public transport 27

Rain Man 34
reading 54, 55, 56–7, 165–7
redirecting attention 150–1
repetitive movements 39, 52, 59
repetitive noises 39, 52
   replacing with words, poems and
      songs 152–4
Reserves (of Body and Soul) 100–2
   Battles and 101, 112, 115, 118
restaurants and cafeterias 19–20,
   75, 150, 173–4
Return of the King, The (cartoon) 50
rituals 66–76, 123
rules of the Earth 193–4, 194–5
Russian
   concept of friendship 156
   rituals 67
   vocabulary list 197
"Russian park" 75

San Diego 32, 96, 108, 173, 195
San Diego Regional Center for the
   Developmentally Disabled 51
San Diego Unified School District
   (SDUSD) 32, 51, 97, 181
schedule boards 73, 77–9
schedules 77–82
   changes 82
   mornings 77–9, 103
   playgrounds 79–81
   weekly 74–6
second grade 55, 189–91
self-blame 11
sensory helpers 97–9
sibling shame 160–4

smiling
  babyhood 13
  smile schedule 79
social interaction
  aggression 23, 53
  inability to share 47
  "playground behavior" schedule
    80–1
  redirecting attention 150–1
  tantrums 53
  see also friendships
social skills 55, 75
"socialization" programs 158–9
sock-laundry 117–19
soda 14
Soviet Union/USSR 42, 66–7, 123,
    172
special-education schooling 17, 51,
    55, 181–4, 189–90
  lack of privacy 98
  vacuum of connections 156–7
specialists 16–17, 38
speech delay 15–16, 38, 39
speech therapy 16
step-by-step instruction books 59
summer school 54–5, 185–8
"support language" 64–5

table manners 172–3
tags (clothing) 94–5
tantrums 24–5, 39, 51, 53, 54, 55,
    175–7
  "buying time" 61–5
  childrens' dislike of 63, 88
  OMAFED and 138–40

public 27–8, 96, 175–7
reasons for 46, 63–4
typical day for three-year-old
    26–30
television 14, 29, 46, 47, 54
  "buying time" 63, 64
  and the Dragon of Negativity
    131
  enforcing rules with OMAFED
    135–6
  family viewing disrupted 18
  snacking in front of 114–16
  trash information 182
toilet training see potty and toilet
    training
toys and non-toys 14–15, 45, 49
transitions 15, 39

Unforgiven 15
United States 16, 67

vocabulary 38, 45, 47
  building with ChOT 91
  at four years old 50, 196–7
  promise ritual 70–2

warming clothes 109–10
warrior-parents 111–13
weather 31, 95–7
well-meaning people 175–80
winning 53, 145